THE
COMING
GREAT
REFORMATION

-- The 1996 Prophecies --

New Insights into the Coming Worldwide
"Shaking", Reformation and Revival

ANDREW STROM

Revival School

The Coming Great Reformation

First published online, 1996
First printing, 2008

Wholesale distribution by Lightning Source, Inc.

Published by: Revival School
www.revivalschool.com
prophetic@revivalschool.com

ISBN-13: 978-0-9799073-2-6

ISBN-10: 0-9799073-2-2

1. Prophets -- History   2. Revival

CONTENTS

Introduction 5

1. Visions of Reformation and Revival 9

2. The Laodicean Church 37

3. Religious Extremes – Legalism vs. License 49

4. Revival! 77

5. The Sin of Rebellion 97

6. Two Revivals? 123

Appendix 147

Bibliography 155

"Learn from me, how difficult a thing it is to throw off errors confirmed by the example of all the world, and which, through long habit, have become a second nature to us."

- MARTIN LUTHER, THE REFORMER.

INTRODUCTION

Back in 1993 I entered a period in my Christian walk of some of the deepest dealings of God that I have ever experienced. Along with this deep dealing came an anointing the like of which I had never before known, even when newly baptized in the Holy Spirit some years before. I would often spend whole evenings just basking in the awesome presence of God, tears coursing down my face, as I beheld Him again, in all His majesty and holiness. The one message that kept coming through again and again at this time was a very simple yet profound one: "Revival is coming!" I had been praying – often agonizingly – for Revival for about ten years up to this point, including seven years of the most shattering "wilderness"-type experience. And suddenly, it seemed literally as though the heavens had opened!

Each time I received anew this promise of "Revival" I sensed that it was an imminent – even urgent – message. And it was at about this time too, that God began to bring me across many other Christians who had been through a similar process to my own – praying and prophetic people from all kinds of backgrounds, each with a similar message from God. A number had even been given amazingly specific dreams and visions concerning what was to come. At that time I had very little idea of what had been said by prophetic ministries overseas about Revival coming to New Zealand, but right from the beginning, I was aware that God was showing us that in order to prepare His people for worldwide Revival on a huge scale, massive 'change' and Reformation would first have to be visited upon His church, just as with many great moves of God in the past. If we expect to be involved in the great last-days 'harvest', then surely it is logical that God would have to bring correspondingly huge 'Reformation' upon His church in order to prepare her for such a harvest? This is especially true if the church is in the kind of inward-looking, 'Laodicean' state that we generally see her in today.

I have been studying Reformation and Revival history now for over twelve years, and when I began to realize what God was saying to us here in New Zealand, I began to write and put out a series of small booklets on the subject. These seemed to produce a "snowball" effect, as more and more people read them and got into contact with me from all over the country. Before long I was in touch with literally hundreds of praying groups and individuals from right across New Zealand (population – three and a half million) and almost all of them, it seemed, were being shown the same things.

Some of the aspects that God has spoken about in detail here in NZ are: The great "shaking" and total Reformation of the church that lie ahead, the incredible "street-church" of tomorrow (a new 'street-based' Revival movement, absolutely saturated with the glory of God), the 'violent' new Revival ministries (apostles and prophets, etc), the powerful, piercing "repentance" preaching with tremendous conviction of sin, the healings and miracles, with thousands of young people gathered in the streets, and the glorious new 'battle' and praise music that He is about to raise up, etc. All of these aspects will be discussed fully in this book.

There will be many who will find the implications of what I am about to share quite shocking at times. This is not surprising. Have you ever heard of a "comfortable" Reformation? For those who have a vested interest in the status quo, true Revival and true Reformation have always been the most "uncomfortable" of sub-jects. And yes, many will be shocked by the picture that I paint within these pages. I believe that we are about to witness the greatest upheaval in the history of the church.

However, there is nothing that will be presented here that has not been thoroughly tested against the precedents and principles found right through the Scriptures and also church history. For over twelve years now, God has led me to study and take careful note of the ways in which He has moved amongst His people in the past, from the beginning of the Old Testament right down through the history of the church. These are the precedents and principles by which we must judge every new movement. There is no such thing as a Revival or new move of God that exists in isolation. Every Revival is built on the foundations laid in previous Revivals. And there are familiar patterns running right through all of the great moves of God that I have studied. Even Jesus felt the need to use the Scriptures to prove the validity of His ministry.

In recent years there has been considerable controversy over the movement known as the "Toronto blessing" and the various manifestations associated with it. This book is certainly not going to be completely spent merely discussing the various arguments for or against this movement. Rather, we will be concentrating on the great Reformation and harvest that lie ahead. However, despite the fact that the Toronto Airport church (home of the 'Toronto Blessing') has now been officially expelled from the Vineyard movement, Toronto is still an important topic in the context of this book. Therefore, I have set aside one chapter in which we will discuss this movement in some detail, using facts from both the Scriptures and church history, plus a number of visions that have been given to praying people in NZ which give insight into it. But like I said, the vast bulk of these pages will be spent discussing the coming great Reformation, Revival and harvest, and our preparation for them.

As well as looking at Reformations and Revivals down through history, we will also be discussing a large number of recent dreams and visions given to praying people in New Zealand. I have no desire that these visions be treated as 'authoritative' in themselves, though I myself certainly believe that they have been given by God. Rather, like anything else, these dreams and visions must be tested to make sure that they line up with the patterns that God has established whenever He has moved in the past. In other words, they must line up with the Scriptures and also with God's established pattern of Reformation and Revival throughout church history. And of course, we must each also ask ourselves, "Does this vision witness with my spirit as truly being of God?"

It is my belief that every one of the dreams and visions described in this book passes each of these tests with flying colors. True Reformation and true Revival have always been the most revolutionary, the most earth-shattering, the most 'violent' spiritual events of their time. It is my belief that we live in the most momentous days in the history of the church. Incredible events are about to unfold before our very eyes. In the many dreams and visions given in New Zealand, God has likened the coming move to a 'Bride', to a warrior army, etc. Of course, such analogies are entirely Scriptural, and they often describe perfectly the role of the coming 'Revival' ministries.

Surely, if we are in the 'last days', then the extraordinary times that we live in call for an unusually powerful and sweeping Revival? And surely, in such times as these, it makes perfect sense that God would send the greatest-ever Reformation in order to prepare His church for what must surely be the greatest 'harvest' (the final one) in all history? We only have to look around us to see the urgent need for such a great move of God. Both the church and the world are desperately poverty-stricken spiritually. And right down through history, God has always brought an outpouring of great mercy before He has brought great judgment. May not this present desperate hour be one of those times?

Chapter One

VISIONS OF REFORMATION AND REVIVAL

For generations now, God has been speaking to His people all over the world about the great end-times Revival, the final "harvest" that will come before the tribulation and judgment that will close this present age. On the day of Pentecost the apostle Peter declared, "And in it shall come to pass in the last days, says God, that I will pour out of My Spirit on ALL FLESH; your sons and your daughters shall prophesy, your young men shall see visions, your old men shall dream dreams" (Acts 2:17). The Bible speaks of the 'former' (or early) rain and also the "latter rain" (or 'harvest-ripening' rain) which occurs much later, just before the wheat fields are harvested. It is this great "latter rain" outpouring of God's Spirit that we are now awaiting.

Jesus spoke of the harvest as being the "end of the age" (Matt 13:39). In the parable of the tares and the wheat He declared that at the time of this end-time harvest He would cause the 'tares' (or false wheat) to be separated from the true wheat. The true wheat would be gathered into His barn, but the false wheat would be gathered into bundles and burnt. We are now living in the days that will see the dramatic fulfillment of this parable, first in the church (for judgment must first begin at the house of God – 1 Peter 4:17) and then in the world. This 'tares and wheat' parable should be a very disturbing and significant one for the end-time church to contemplate, and in many ways it is central to some of the awesome (and sometimes shocking) things that God has shown us here in New Zealand regarding the immediate future of the church.

Some Christians have opposed the idea that there will be any great Revival at the end of the age. They point out that according to the

Scriptures, the end-times church will be in a state of almost complete spiritual bankruptcy – materialistic, carnal, lukewarm – "lovers of pleasures more than lovers of God". Surely such a church would be in no state to bring in such a great 'harvest' in Jesus' name? And in this respect we have to admit that WHAT THEY ARE SAYING IS ABSOLUTELY REASONABLE AND CORRECT. Indeed, the Scriptures on the subject are universal in the picture they paint of an end-times church that is virtually apostate and Laodicean in every respect. How can such a church ever be part of the greatest Revival in history? The answer to this question is very simple: IT CAN'T!

Just as with many previous moves of God right down through the ages, God has made it very clear that once again, only a "remnant" of believers, who have willingly gone through the necessary preparation, will have a part in the coming Revival. Those who refuse to submit to this preparation process, preferring to remain in their present 'Laodicean' state – will clearly have no part whatsoever in the coming move of God. Rather, just as Jesus has promised, the lukewarm are to be "spewed" out of the mouth of God (Rev 3:16).

The Bible makes it very clear that God cannot live with a 'blessings'-obsessed, Laodicean-type church. And in this world of increasing darkness, it becomes doubly imperative that God has a people in the earth who are shining forth His light with the greatest possible effectiveness. This is what the coming Reformation is all about – finding and cleansing and anointing such a people so that they can shine forth His light in all the earth. This is why such a massive 'shaking' and repentance must first come upon the church. God must find and raise up such a people.

And as always, only a "remnant" who embraces this dealing of God will make it through into the coming move, just as only a remnant of the Israelites who left Egypt made it through into the Promised Land. The rest were overthrown by God in the wilderness. We live in the most awesome of days – the days of separation, judgment and "harvest" spoken about in Mt 13:24-43.

And this entire process must first begin in God's own house (1 Pe 4:17).

It is interesting to note in the parable of the tares and the wheat (Mt 13), that at the end of the age it is the 'false wheat' in God's kingdom that is bundled together (unified) first and separated from the true wheat. When this separating process is complete, we see God's judgment fall upon these 'tares'. As history clearly shows, God is very patient, but the time must come for the 'sifting' and judgment of His people. While there is still true wheat amongst the tares, the tares are relatively safe. But as soon as this separating process is complete, the tares are in imminent danger of falling under the judgment fire of God's holy wrath. He will not forever stand for a people who cause His name to be mocked and brought into an open shame.

Meanwhile, God's true remnant will be purified, tried as by fire, until every impurity is gone – prepared as a Bride fit for her King – pure and holy, "not having spot or wrinkle or any such thing" (Eph 5:27). This will be the company of saints who will bring in the great last-days harvest of souls, and who will preach the gospel of the kingdom in all the earth with great authority and power, and with signs and wonders following, before the end comes.

AN OPEN VISION OF THE BRIDE OF CHRIST

The following is a vision that was given to a friend of mine who is very experienced in this 'prophetic' area, late in 1993. This gentleman has many years of Christian ministry behind him, and in the last few years has been given a number of stunning dreams and visions about the coming move of God. However, he told me that this particular vision was one of the most powerful of all. It unfolded before his eyes like a movie in Technicolor, with God speaking to him about aspects of it as he watched.

Basically, it was a traditional wedding scene. The radiantly beautiful Bride had just stepped out of the Cathedral and was standing on the top step, just outside. My friend was told that the Bride was LEAVING 'CHRISTENDOM' (AND ALL THAT GOES WITH IT) FOREVER, leaving the 'church' system behind. The Groom (who was Jesus) took her arm, so that He could lead her down and proudly display His beautiful Bride to all the world.

Still inside the Cathedral were all the relatives (these were the various 'streams' and denominations of the church as we know it). Suddenly, while the Bride was still on the top step, an invisible hand gave her a beautiful lily (which had been plucked out by the roots). This was her bridal 'bouquet' (her new anointing, perhaps?) and for some reason it seemed to be given to her rather late. She threw this bouquet backwards, and some of her relatives in the church, who had been watching her with great jealousy and awe, made a grab for the bouquet. Two of them seemed to snatch it up. The Groom then led the Bride down the steps and through the huge crowd of cheering people down below, who had been unable to get into the Cathedral. In a later vision, my friend was shown that after they had made their way through this huge throng, the happy couple were then taken away on their honeymoon, which was to last for a thousand years.

When speaking of the 'end of the age', Jesus Himself often used 'wedding'-type analogies. In the parable of the five wise and the five foolish virgins, for instance (which is again obviously referring to CHRISTIANS), Jesus again divides the believers into two groups. When the watchman cries, "Behold, the Bridegroom cometh; go ye out to meet Him!", fully HALF of the (supposedly 'Spirit-filled') Christians suddenly find that there is a severe lack of "oil" in their lamps! Because of this, they are completely shut out of the marriage feast. Again, in Jesus' parable of the wedding feast (Mt 22:1-14), the King sends out His servants to tell those who have been 'invited' that everything is now ready, and that it is time to come and celebrate His Son's marriage. But these 'invited' ones make light of it, maltreating His servants and refusing to attend. The King then sends His armies to destroy their city and raze it to the ground, and sends out His servants once again, into the highways and byways, compelling everybody, 'both good and bad' to come in and rejoice with Him at the marriage of His Son.

Like that last parable, I believe that we now live in days of tremendous danger for those who have already received their 'invitations' to the coming wedding feast. As in every Revival, many who have been invited, many who 'should be there', never make it, and their places are taken by the unknowns, the outcasts, the meek, the despised and the rejected. So let those who have 'reputations' to protect, those who are counted amongst the "wise and prudent", those who are seen as 'somebodies' – let them all beware! For these are days not only of great opportunity, but also of great danger. "For many are called, but few are chosen" (Mt 22:14).

It is my belief that God is going to delight in using the "foolish things of this world to confound the wise" in this Revival. As always, He is going to use the "little" people – the people who are of no account – to humble the powerful, the successful and the mighty. He is going to take the unknowns and the outcasts, the praying solo mothers and the ex-gang-members, the "fishermen and the tax-collectors", and He is going to anoint them and raise them up into the mightiest army of miracle-working apostles, prophets, evangelists, etc, that this world has ever known. And all they will be interested in doing is glorifying Him in every conceivable way.

When this happens, many of today's Christian leaders will marvel, just as the scribes and Chief Priests 'marveled' at the boldness of Peter and John when they saw that they were "uneducated and untrained men, they marveled. And they realized that THEY HAD BEEN WITH JESUS" (Acts 4:13). That is the secret: "THEY HAD BEEN WITH JESUS". And thus it will be of everyone that is used of God in this Revival. "I thank You, Father, Lord of heaven and earth, that You have hidden these things from the wise and prudent and have revealed them to babes" (Mt 11:25).

I believe that many forgotten and hidden Christians, whom God has been quietly preparing for many years, will make up this radiantly lovely Bride of Christ in these last days. Like a hidden army, they will suddenly spring forth as if from nowhere, to take the field in the name of the Lord and of righteousness. Thus it has always been, and always will be, with the greatest moves of God. Hidden preparation and sudden, aggressive mobilization have been the keys to many of God's greatest victories in the past, and this time will be no different.

Be assured of this: Jesus must have His virgin Bride. He cannot return until a Bride is prepared for Him that is literally "without spot, or wrinkle, or any such thing". That is what this Revival is all about: to bring into being and display His beautiful Bride to all the world. In physical terms, this 'Bridal' company of saints will not look particularly amazing or special. Like the original apostles, they will be ordinary people with an extraordinary calling and anointing. Many of them will no doubt seem a little rough or 'ill-suited' (from an outward point of view) to be endued with such power, but this will only serve to bring God all the more glory. They may not look like much on the outside, but these men and women will have hearts that are literally "as pure as snow". They will be a people who know exactly what it means to walk in total heart purity before God. To Him, they will be vastly more precious than all of the "gold or pearls or costly array" of this entire Universe. And they will go forth with great power, "destroying the works of the devil" in His name.

THE INCREDIBLE "STREET-CHURCH" OF TOMORROW

For the past fifteen years or more, all over the world God has been warning His people of the great "shaking" and Reformation that are about to come upon His church. In 1982, for instance, in a very powerful visitation, one well-known American intercessor/leader was clearly spoken to by God: "I am going to change the understanding and expression of Christianity IN THE EARTH in one generation". As we have seen in the vision of the Bride, she was seen leaving 'Christendom' (and all that goes with it) forever – leaving behind the 'church system' as we know it. From this and many other visions and prophecies, etc, in New Zealand, it has become obvious to us that IN ORDER TO BE PART OF THE NEW MOVE OF GOD IT WILL BE NECESSARY TO COMPLETELY LEAVE TODAY'S CHURCH SYSTEM. This is not "rebellion". (In fact we will discuss the subtle dangers of rebellion later in this book). What God has said to us in this regard actually has a tremendous amount of historic precedent, both in Scripture and in church history, as we shall see. The reasons and the timing for this move will become much clearer as we go along.

Of course, those with a vested interest in maintaining the present church hierarchies and systems will be violently opposed to such an idea. Many reformers, such as Martin Luther, John Wesley and William Booth faced enormous opposition from the established church leadership of their day for precisely this reason. This is why true Reformation and Revival are often the most controversial and the most persecuted spiritual events of their time. And this is also why it has often been the CHRISTIANS (particularly the leaders) who have persecuted new moves of God the worst.

Something that God has made very clear to us in NZ is that the coming Revival is to be a "street-based" (or 'open-air' based) move of God. Today we have a "meetings and buildings" oriented church, a church that is hidden away in 'boxes' from the eyes of the world. But, like the early church (where they met daily in the huge open-air temple courtyard – probably the most public place in all Jerusalem), and also like the mighty Wesley and Salvation Army Revivals, the coming move of God is to be truly street-based. (There will also, like the early church, be gatherings of the saints from "house to house" (Acts 2:41-47)).

God is also going to use this Reformation and Revival to smash down the dividing walls that separate the Christians. Jesus has never stopped desiring that there be only "one" undivided body. Today, however, just amongst the Pentecostal/Charismatic Christians alone there are so many divisions, "streams" and denominations that it is almost impossible to count them all. Each division has its own 'label', and in many ways they operate like competing corporations, selling the same "product" under different labels (with slight variations). It's ridiculous! And the whole church system today is set up in such a way that it just ensures that these divisions continue. These are 'structural' divisions that have been virtually set in concrete – "institutionalized" divisions that are simply accepted and perpetuated by each new generation of Christians.

God is going to smash down these 'walls' in this Revival. How? By bringing His people out from underneath all these "labels"! In one very significant vision several years ago, a NZ prophet saw God firing "flaming arrows" into the churches. These flaming arrows were 'on-fire' ministries, speaking the word of God. However, the Pastors were rushing around trying to damp down the flames! God then sent a "mighty wind" to fan the flames, and suddenly the doors of the churches burst open and all the people flooded out onto the streets to become one huge throng. I believe that this is an exact picture of what is about to take place, and in many ways it also illustrates the whole concept of "Reformation" very well (as will be seen from later chapters).

Another local intercessor was also shown a vision relating to this several years ago, while deep in prayer. The first thing she saw was church buildings of every kind – stained glass, steeples, plain and modern, etc. This part of the vision was in black and white. The churches all looked abandoned – like a ghost town, with birds nesting in them and doors and windows askew, etc. And in each church, the intercessor saw a huge old curtain or 'veil' that was in absolute tatters.

The second part of the vision was all in color. She saw hundreds of Christians outdoors (with guitars, etc) fellowshipping together in the open air. She knew that these Christians had abandoned their church buildings and 'divisions', and were now fellowshipping freely out-of-doors. When she asked God what the huge tattered curtain in each of the abandoned churches represented, she was told that when Jesus was crucified, the veil/curtain in the temple was rent, thus allowing the people free access to the 'holy of holies'. However, the churches had risen up this veil once again. But now these structures had been abandoned, thus allowing the common people free access to God's holy-of-holies once more. What an astounding vision!

One of the best examples I know of a truly "street-based" Revival movement was the early Salvation Army (1860's to the 1890's). In those days, the Salvationists were largely a bunch of 'on-fire', praying zealots, given to holding open-air street meetings in which their brass bands would crash away raucously and their preachers would exhort the people to repentance under a mighty anointing. Their motto was, "Go for souls, and go for the worst!" Many early Salvationists were arrested, and there were often full-scale riots involving huge mobs, etc. The newspapers were full of it. The Salvationists were both controversial and notorious. And thousands upon thousands of people were converted. Within days of the first tiny contingent of Salvationists arriving in New Zealand, the following cable-gram was dispatched to General Booth in England: "Dunedin, Auckland blazing. Christchurch shortly. Reinforce sharp."

There can be no doubt that God desires a loving, militant "street-level" Church today. After all, isn't that what the early church was all about? I believe that it will become common for incredible signs, wonders and miracles to be performed on the streets as a result of this coming Revival. In fact, I believe that we are about to see a demonstration of God's glory in the area of the miraculous that will be even more powerful than the book of Acts.

Enormous love, enormous boldness and 'joy unspeakable' will be just some of the characteristics of this Revival. And everything will be bathed in prayer. In fact this Revival is going to be BUILT on prayer. As Charles Finney said, "Revival comes from heaven when heroic souls enter the conflict determined to win or die... 'The kingdom of heaven suffereth violence and the violent take it by force.'" There is no substitute for faith-filled, Spirit-fired "agonizing" prayer. Only those who are prepared and praying will be involved in this Revival from the beginning. As history shows, great blessing can only ever fall when the people of God learn to seek His face with all their heart.

THE "VIOLENT" NEW MINISTRIES

Along with the picture of a radiantly beautiful Bride, God has also often likened the coming move to an army being prepared for battle, and then attacking the enemy with great violence. I myself believe that spiritual aggression and daring faith are all part and parcel of the Bride's radiant beauty. She will "love not her life unto the death" (Rev 12:11). All over the world, there have been numerous dreams and visions that speak of the great army of God that is about to arise and do battle.

About two years ago, for instance, a New Zealand prophet was given a vision of the 'vanguard' of the army (those at the front), who were in a long column advancing slowly towards the enemy with measured steps. They were slowly forcing the enemy back, but the reason they didn't rush forward into battle was because they were waiting for the rest of the army behind them to get into formation so that they could all rush forward together. In this vision, there was a sudden 'roar', like a great shout of victory, and the whole army suddenly charged forward into battle, utterly decimating the enemy with a great slaughter. This went on for some time. Suddenly the prophet realized that in the vision, Satan himself was now isolated and completely surrounded by the armies of God. And there was a sudden awareness that Jesus was now present, and that Satan was about to be bound in chains and cast into the abyss.

While I am certainly not a believer in 'dominion theology' or other extreme teachings, it cannot be denied that the Bible clearly states in Heb 10:12-13: "But this Man (Christ), after He had offered on sacrifice for sins forever, sat down at the right hand of God, from that time waiting till His enemies are made His footstool." It seems clear from this and other Scriptures, that Jesus is waiting at the right hand of the Father until His enemies are defeated and placed 'under His feet'. Of course, in a very real way, the devil is already a defeated foe, having been defeated by Christ at Calvary. However, it seems that he has remained in his position as the "prince of this world" for the time being. Isn't it logical that in the last days God would raise up an army of believers who would truly enforce Christ's victory over His enemies (as the Scriptures declare)?

It is my belief that the army of God that is now in the final stages of preparation on the earth will pursue the devil's forces across whole continents, razing his strongholds to the ground, laying waste to all his works, and slaughtering his armies across a broad front. This will truly be a people that will "destroy the works of the devil" with exceeding violence. After all, did not Jesus Himself say, "I will build my Church, and the gates of hell shall not prevail (Greek: 'stand strong') against it"? The gates of hell simply cannot stand against the Church that Jesus builds! We are to smash down the gates and invade Satan's territory, destroying every devilish work as we go. We are to be a "violent" people, fiercely intent (as Joshua's people were) on "taking the kingdom by force".

The following is a dream that was given to a prophet friend of mine, who has received a large number of stunning dreams and visions about the coming move of God over the past four years or so. This particular dream was given to him four times. It is probably the most 'unusual' one that he has ever been given, but he knows that it is of God. I believe that it may well give us vital insight into God's battle strategy for the last days. The first thing that he saw was what seemed to be fallen angelic princes, drifting high above the earth. Though they were obviously very evil, they had the appearance of loving, 'saintly' angels. They appeared to be gloating at the ease with which they held sway over the people of the earth. Under their direct command were much uglier beings with huge swords – the 'strongmen' over nations – who were sent down to earth literally to cause men to kill one another, to make them willing to lay down their lives for nationalistic causes, etc.

Basically, these 'strongmen' would use any possible means to cause human beings to die young, particularly on a large scale.

Now here comes the really bizarre part. It appeared in the dream that somehow, the highest demonic princes were able to 'feed' on the spiritual life that was released when these people were killed. It was brought up to them in the form of 'manna' by the strongmen. In the dream, my friend heard the fallen princes say to the strongmen, "Go down and kill as many humans as you can, for it is the last days, and we must store up as much 'manna' as possible before the end." Suddenly, in the dream, a spaceship appeared, full of mighty men and women of God. They saw exactly what was going on, and for a while they tried to warn the people of the earth. However, this achieved very little, so they mounted a direct attack against the strongmen. They didn't bother with the lower-ranked demons. They went directly for the 'palace' in the heavens in which the strongmen themselves were based.

When the spaceship reached this palace, the captain and the other leaders (the 'five-fold' ministries) from the ship stormed into the palace, leaving behind a support crew. Using space-age weapons (hand-held lasers, etc) they attacked the strongmen with deadly skill and great daring. These were highly trained specialists. They worked as a team, and they were utterly fearless in battle. The strongmen were terrified. They were trying to kill the five-fold ministries with their swords (not their guns for some reason), but were unable to do so. The strongmen were destroyed one by one, and soon the corridors were littered with their dead bodies. The demonic princes over them were panic-stricken, knowing that their support and protection was fast evaporating. It was a total rout, a complete victory for God.

Now some of you may have found the above dream a little 'unusual', to say the least. However, when my friend, who was given this dream four times, prayed about it, he realized that some of the concepts contained in it would have been almost impossible to understand if they had not been put across in such a way. I have noticed that in dreams and visions, God often uses the most simple illustrations to shed light on the most profound truths. I believe that this dream and others like it, give significant insight into the great spiritual war that is about to be waged.

We are told in Heb 12:26, "...but now He has promised, saying, 'Yet once more I will shake not only the earth but also heaven.'" And in Rev 12:7-9 we read: "And war broke out in heaven: Michael and his angels fought with the dragon; and the dragon and his angels fought, but they did not prevail, nor was a place found for them in heaven any longer. So the great dragon was cast out, that serpent of old, called the Devil and Satan, who deceives the whole world; he was cast to the earth, and his angels were cast out with him."

I believe that the dream recounted earlier is speaking of the vital role that the end-times ministries will also play in this victory over Satan. We can tell that humans (not just angels) will have an integral part in this victory because just two verses later we read: "And they overcame him by the blood of the Lamb, and by the word of their testimony, and they did not love their lives to the death" (Rev 12:11). I do not believe that what is spoken of in the dream is merely a 'prayer' battle – to be fought out by the intercessors (though prayer will be vital, of course. In fact, the battle must be won in prayer first). Rather, I believe that somehow, in the coming Revival, when the new ministries have been raised up and anointed by God, there will be direct confrontations between certain of these 'five-fold' ministries and the 'strongmen over nations' that we have spoken of.

When these strongmen have been destroyed, and Satan and the rest of his angels have been cast down to earth by God's angelic armies, then I believe we will see the period on earth known as the "Great Tribulation", where unprecedented deception, darkness and persecution will arise. Right through the last days 'harvest' period, I believe that there will be persecution, earthquakes, natural disasters, 'wars and rumors of wars', etc. But when the real Tribulation begins, darkness and persecution will greatly increase. In fact, I believe that many Christians will be imprisoned and killed towards the end. "...Woe to the inhabitants of the earth and the sea! For the devil has come down to you, having great wrath, because he knows that he has a short time" (Rev 12:12).

It is clear that the entire Bride of Christ will be actively "destroying the works of the devil" at various levels, in the coming Revival. But what exactly are these 'works of the devil'? To me, they are anything that keeps people bound in sin, misery, sickness or oppression. Jesus said that the 'thief' comes to "steal, and to kill, and to destroy. I have come that they may have life, and that they might have it more abundantly" (Jn 10:10). So how exactly did Jesus 'destroy the works of the devil' from out of peoples' lives in His day? Well, one obvious aspect of Jesus' ministry was His consistent preaching of a very strong and direct repentance message. He also said of His ministry, "The blind see and the lame walk; the lepers are cleansed and the deaf hear; the dead are raised up and the poor have the gospel preached to them" (Mt 11:5). Truly, His was a ministry of forgiveness, cleansing and liberation aimed especially at the poor, the sick, the broken-hearted, and all who were 'oppressed of the devil'.

At times, Jesus also found it necessary to bring a "searing rebuke", because of the hardness of heart present in a group or an individual. Obviously, at such times He perceived that a piercing, anointed word of rebuke was the only thing that would break down the strongholds of sin, compromise, religion, unbelief, etc, that were holding these people captive.

One thing that seems to have been coming through again and again in NZ, is the fact that the army that God is now preparing will attack the kingdom of darkness with incredible violence – with reckless daring and ruthless aggression. They will make no 'treaties' and they will take no prisoners. In one way, as we have discussed, I believe that Jesus is waiting at the right hand of the Father until His enemies are made a 'footstool' for His feet. In another, very real way, He will truly be with us by His Spirit, triumphantly leading His people into war.

A prophet friend of mine, who until recently has only rarely received dreams or visions, was given a particularly powerful vision about two years ago. He said that it was so real that it was literally just like being there. This vision only lasted a short time, but it had a very powerful impact on him. What he saw was this: He was standing in what appeared to be a valley, staring at something the size of a mountain that had just burst up through the surface of the earth. But this was no mere volcanic eruption. What my friend saw was, in fact, the head of a gigantic white horse that had literally burst up through the ground. Around its head, molten lava was spurting. My friend said that he was frightened by the look of sheer ferocity in the eyes of the creature. There could be no denying that this was truly a 'war' horse, fiercely intent on the battle to come.

One of the things that strike me as very significant about this vision is the fact that THE WHITE HORSE'S HEAD HAS NOW BROKEN THROUGH THE SURFACE OF THE EARTH. "... and behold, a white horse. He who sat on it had a bow; and a crown was given to him, and he went out conquering and to conquer" (Rev 6:2). "Now I saw heaven opened, and behold, a white horse. And He who sat on him was called Faithful and True, and in righteousness He judges and makes war... and His name is called The Word of God. And the armies in heaven, clothed in fine linen, white and clean, followed Him on white horses" (Rev 19:11-14).

All over the world in the past fifteen years or so, God has been speaking of a distinct grouping of ministries that would again arise in great power in the last days. These are the end-times "Elijah" ministries, who are about to be raised up, as prophesied for thousands of years, under a mighty anointing, "preparing the way of the Lord" and making straight 'a highway for our God' (Is 40:3). As we are told in Mal 4:5-6, "Behold, I will send you Elijah the prophet before the coming of the great and dreadful day of the LORD: And he will turn the hearts of the fathers to the children, and the hearts of the children to their fathers, lest I come and strike the earth with a curse." Jesus Himself stated that "Elijah comes, and will restore all things..." (Mt 17:11).

There are at least three great men of God in history who have walked under this mighty mantle and anointing of Elijah: Elijah himself, the prophet Elisha, and also John the Baptist (who came 'preparing the way of the Lord' at His first coming). Now that we are approaching Christ's return – the "great and dreadful day of the Lord", we can expect that God will once again raise up bold and anointed messengers, just as prophesied, who will go forth 'in the spirit and power of Elijah', preparing the way of the Lord once more. "And this gospel of the kingdom will be preached in all the world as a witness to all the nations, and then the end will come" (Mt 24:14).

To get some idea of the rugged and even 'violent' nature of these Elijah ministries, it is necessary to go back and look at the 'Elijahs' of the past. There is no question that these were blunt, uncompromising, fearless messengers of God. They attacked the sin and compromise of their day with cutting power, for the full authority of the Living God was behind every word that they spoke. Their words were like a consuming fire, a piercing two-edged sword, a 'hammer that breaks the rock into pieces'. And they stood unbending in the name of truth and of righteousness, to put to flight God's enemies, to rebuke His wayward people, and to again lift up His 'standard' amidst the darkness of their time.

Witness the fearless prophet Elijah on top of Mt Carmel (1 Kings 18). At his word there has not been one drop of rain in all Israel for three and a half years. And now here he is, the only man who dares openly oppose the evil Baal-worshipping empire under cruel queen/witch Jezebel. Hear Elijah lay down his mocking challenge to the Baal priests and prophets: "Perhaps your god is on a journey. Or perhaps he sleeps and needs awakening!" (v27). And then, at the time of the evening sacrifice, we see Elijah, that fearless prophet of God call fire down from heaven right before the startled eyes of all present. "Now when all the people saw it, they fell on their faces; and they said, 'The LORD, He is God; The LORD, He is God'. And Elijah said to them, 'Seize the prophets of Baal! Do not let one of them escape!' So they seized them: And Elijah brought them down to the brook Kishon, and executed them there" (v 39-40).

Now we jump to 2 Kings Chapter one. The rebellious and evil king of Samaria has just sent fifty soldiers to bring the prophet Elijah down from the hill on which he sits. "And Elijah answered and said to the captain of fifty, if I be a man of God, then let fire come down from heaven, and consume you and your fifty. And there came down fire from heaven, and consumed him and his fifty" (v10). Rather foolishly, the king then sends another fifty soldiers to bring Elijah down. These too are consumed by fire in exactly the same way. It is not until the next captain of fifty comes to him on his knees, begging and pleading, that Elijah agrees to go down with him to see the king.

The above incidents, which are typical of the kinds of things that took place in the lives of both Elijah and Elisha, demonstrate not only their power and authority under God, but also the spiritually 'violent' nature of this kind of ministry. One Scripture that has been given to myself and others again and again in relation to the new move of God is Mt 11:12: "... from the days of John the Baptist until now the kingdom of heaven suffers violence, and the violent take it by force." I believe that the entire coming Revival worldwide is to be a spiritually 'violent' move – probably the most aggressive that this planet has ever seen. The 'Elijah' ministries will lead God's armies into battle – a glorious army, "terrible with banners", and no weapon that is formed against them will stand.

Who could doubt that we live today on the verge of the most momentous days in the history of the church? The Revival that is coming will surely be the greatest outpouring of the Holy Spirit that the world has ever known. It will be "the former rain and the latter rain in the first month, and the floors shall be full of wheat, and the vats shall overflow with wine and oil" (Joel 2:23-24). We live in a time when God's mighty 'men and women of valor' will once again roam the earth, and when "the people who do know their God shall be strong and do exploits" (Dan 11:32). The apostles, prophets and evangelists that are about to arise in these

- 25 -

last days, will be amongst the most anointed warriors of God that have ever trod the earth. They will literally walk in the resurrection glory of Jesus Christ. Endued with 'power from on high', they will go forth, a fearful army, "conquering and to conquer", and nothing will stand in their path.

APOSTOLIC TEACHINGS AND PRACTICES

Like the early Church, the new move of God is to be built on the 'foundation' of the soon-to-emerge mighty "apostles and prophets" that He is about to raise up for this hour (Eph 2:20). This is to be an 'apostolic' move. As it was in the beginning, so it will be also at the end. Just as with every great move of God, this one is to be built around the new leadership that He is raising up specifically for this hour. Thus it will clearly be "WHEN THE NEW APOSTLES ARISE" that true Reformation and Revival will begin. It is these 'apostolic' ministries who will be the 'violent' ministries, raised up by God as Joshua was, to lead His people into war – to "take the kingdom by force". And with the return of true apostolic leadership will come a restoration of many basic "book- of-Acts" type apostolic teachings and practices.

One of the most basic and obvious of these apostolic teachings, I believe, will be to restore the original meaning and purpose of the Lord's Supper and also Believer's Baptism. Both of these are seen by many Christians merely as something akin to a symbolic ritual, performed in 'rememberance' or just out of obedience to Scripture, rather than because they have tremendous spiritual impact from God's point of view. In reality, there is actually NOTHING that Jesus has instituted in the New Testament that is merely a "symbolic" act or a 'ritual' that we are to perform. Such things belong to the Old Covenant, not the New. Everything that Jesus has instituted in the New Covenant has tremendous spiritual value and life-giving power, if only we can partake of these things by faith, as He intended.

When we partake of the Lord's Supper, we are supposed to be partaking afresh of the "bread of life" (the word of God) and the cleansing power of the "blood of the new covenant" (see Mt 26:26-28, Jn 6:48-58, 1 Cor 10:16-17, 1 Cor 11:23-30, etc). We are to take this fresh impartation of spiritual life to ourselves by faith, as we eat and drink of the Lord's Supper. Why do you think the early Christians partook of the Lord's Supper "daily" in their gatherings 'from house to house'? And why do you think Paul warned the Corinthians that some of them were 'weak' and others had died because they had not discerned the "one body" that they were to be partakers of, and were therefore "eating and drinking judgment" upon themselves (1 Cor 11:27-33)? There is real spiritual power in the Lord's Supper! This is not just some symbolic ceremony. We are clearly to be continual partakers of the "one body" of Christ, broken for us (and divided amongst us at Communion), and also the cleansing, empowering "blood of the new covenant".

Believer's Baptism (by immersion) is another thing that has lost its true significance over the centuries. We are told often that this is essentially a "symbolic" death-and-burial ceremony for the believer. There are many believers today (even 'Spirit- filled' ones) who think so little of baptism that they haven't even "got around to it yet" at all. But what is God's view of believer's baptism? Does He regard it merely as 'an outward symbol'? I think not! We are told in Rom 6:3-6, "Do you not know that all of us who have been baptized into Christ Jesus were baptized into His death? We were buried therefore with him by baptism into death... We know that our old self was crucified with him so that the sinful body might be destroyed, and we might no longer be enslaved to sin." It is clear from this and many other Scriptures that from a spiritual point of view, baptism is an event of tremendous impact and importance.

Can we claim to have truly "died with Christ" if we have not been baptized by immersion? No, we cannot. Can we claim to have been spiritually 'cut off' from our sinful body, so that we might no longer be enslaved to sin? No, scripturally we cannot. And how else can we "reckon" ourselves to be 'dead to sin'? I believe that rather than being some kind of "symbolic" death, God sees believer's baptism as being a very "literal" spiritual death – a 'cutting off' of the sinful body of the believer. Why else would Peter tell the assembled crowd on the day of Pentecost, "Repent, AND BE BAPTISED in the name of Jesus Christ FOR THE FORGIVENESS OF YOUR SINS..."? (Acts 2:38). And why else would Paul be told, on the day of his conversion, "Arise and BE BAPTISED, AND WASH AWAY YOUR SINS, calling on the name of the Lord"? (Acts 22:16). And what exactly did Jesus mean when He declared that, "Unless a man is BORN OF WATER AND OF THE SPIRIT he cannot enter into the kingdom of God"? (Jn 3:5. See also Mk 16:16-18, 1 Cor 10:1-2, Gal 3:27, Col 2:11-12, Titus 3:5, 1 Pe 3:20-21, etc).

Today, when people want to become a Christian, they are told to simply "ask Jesus into their heart", or "give their heart to the Lord". You might be surprised to learn that there is literally NOT ONE example of anyone in the New Testament being told to do anything like this at all. For instance, there are many, many examples in the book of Acts of people becoming Christians, and yet NOT ONCE are any of them told anything that even remotely resembles, "Just give your heart to the Lord". Instead, people in Bible days were told, "Repent, and be baptized... and you shall receive the gift of the Holy Spirit" (Acts 2:38. See also Acts 8:12-20, Acts 8:35-39, Acts 10:44-48, Acts 19:1-6, Acts 22:16, etc). In the coming Revival, just like the book of Acts, repentance, water-baptism (by immersion) and baptism in the Holy Spirit will be expected to occur IMMEDIATELY someone believes the gospel. Until all of these things have occurred, they will simply not be considered a true, New Testament Christian. This is clearly the only tenable Scriptural position on the matter. What a shockingly inadequate and unscriptural gospel the church has been preaching up until now!

I believe that another huge change in emphasis that will come in with the new move of God will be in the area of sacrificial giving to the poor. In the book of Acts the writer (Luke) devotes a tremendous amount of space to the way in which the early believers sold any excess land, houses or possessions, and gave to the poor (especially to the orphans and widows, etc). From the space that Luke devotes to this subject it is clear that this was a major emphasis of the early Church. And of course, it had always been a major emphasis of JESUS in the first place! To the 'rich young man', Jesus had said, "Sell what you have, and give to the poor, and you will have treasure in heaven; and come, follow me" (Mk 10:21). To his disciples He had said, "Sell your possessions and give alms" (Lk 12:33), and, "How hardly shall they that have riches enter into the kingdom of God!" (Mk 10:23). And to the multitudes who accompanied Him He had said: "Whoever of you does not renounce all that he has cannot be my disciple" (Lk 14:33).

If we are to follow the clear teaching of Jesus, then we are to renounce ownership of all that we have, and our possessions are to literally become God's, to do with as He wills. It is interesting to note that after Jesus had eaten with Zacchaeus the Tax Collector, the little man declared, "Behold, Lord, the HALF OF MY GOODS I GIVE TO THE POOR, and if I have defrauded anyone of anything, I restore it fourfold" (Lk 19:8). This was the fruit of genuine repentance in Zacchaeus' life.

You have to admit, none of this sounds like much of a "prosperity" doctrine, does it?

And now we come to the book of Acts, where the apostles passed on the clear teachings of Jesus concerning riches and possessions, to the new converts: "And all who believed were together, and had all things in common; and they sold their possessions and goods and distributed them to all, as any had need" (Acts 2:45). "There was not a needy person among them, for as many as were possessors of lands or houses sold them, and brought the proceeds of what was sold and laid it at the apostles feet; and distribution was made to each as any had need" (Acts 4:34-35). What a tremendous demonstration of brotherly unity and love! For, as Jesus had said, "By this shall all men know that you are my disciples, if you have love one for another" (Jn 13:35). Such sacrificial giving must always 'come from the heart'. It must never

- 29 -

be 'forced' or legalistic. However, as the Scriptures clearly show, giving of this kind really has to be a major emphasis of any true "Revival" movement. And I am convinced that it certainly will be, in the coming move of God.

The above are just some of the more obvious and fundamental apostolic teachings that I believe will be restored in the coming Revival. These are not obscure doctrinal points. They involve some of the most basic and fundamental questions of the New Testament: What do we tell people to do to become a Christian? Why do people need to be baptized in water? Why do we partake of the Lord's Supper? What does Jesus require us to do with our possessions? All of these are PRACTICAL questions which impacted hugely on the everyday life of the early Church. No doubt there will be other fundamental teachings that will also be restored, when the new apostles arise to establish a true "New Testament" Church once again, in our time.

THE "NEW MUSIC"

About nine years ago I became greatly inspired by things that God was showing me about the early Salvation Army Revivals. My wife and I are both musicians, and God began to particularly draw our attention to the concept of anointed "street-music" – a kind of "Revival" music, to be taken out onto the streets just as the early Salvation Army had done a century before. As I have said previously, in those early days the Salvationists were a bunch of on-fire, praying zealots (mostly very young), who took the world by storm with a street-based Christianity totally unlike anything that was around at that time. The early Salvation Army was truly a 'Revival' movement in every sense of the word – born out of the great Awakening of 1859-60 in Britain. And they carried this tremendous 'Revival' anointing with them, out onto the streets.

One of the most controversial aspects of this new movement was the rather loud, "uncouth" praise-music that they employed in their street meetings. What they had done, in fact, was to take the 'pub' music – the 'drinking' music of their day, and transform it into loud, glorious praise music that the street-level people of those times absolutely loved (though you can imagine the storm of controversy in religious circles!). However, there was really nothing new in this concept. Martin Luther and John Wesley, as well as William Booth, have been credited with the saying, "Why should the devil have all the best music?" Street-level Revival requires street-level praise music! If it utterly glorifies God, what does it matter if it is a little 'noisy'? (Actually, one eyewitness commented of an early Salvation Army band that, "It sounds as if a brass band's gone out of its mind!") This was truly 'battle' music – a call to repentance and to war.

Having been so inspired by all of this when I first read up on it, I photocopied some of the information and gave it to other Christian musicians that we knew at the time. My wife and I also became more and more involved in music, and in 1989 we began our first street-band. However, it was clear from the outset that we were lacking the most important thing of all – the "Revival" anointing that the Salvationists had had. Despite this, the whole concept had taken hold in my heart so strongly that I just couldn't leave it alone. I KNEW that it was of God. Perhaps it was just the timing that was wrong?

In 1992 we finally gave up on the whole idea. Less than one year later, however, we received some amazing confirmation from a source that we had never come across before. In the meantime, too, God had taken me through a massive overhaul of my entire Christian walk, and I had come under a prophetic anointing the like of which I had never before experienced. The confirmation we received in 1993 came in the form of a taped message by American preacher James Ryle, who had been given a series of dreams and visions several years earlier which spoke at length of the new "street-music" that would arise with the coming Revival. What amazing and specific confirmation these tapes were! I was literally in tears as I listened to them.

It was after this that I began to learn that God was speaking to a number of prophetic people in NZ about the coming "new music" also. One local intercessor was given the same amazing vision on three separate occasions while deep in prayer. In it, she saw thousands upon thousands of (mostly young) people gathered in the streets, praising God with all their might to a new, modern kind of praise-music. Non-Christians coming near would fall to their knees under great conviction; the presence of God was so strong. This anointed vision was so real that the intercessor wept whenever she received it. She believes that its fulfillment is very near now.

Another NZ prophet was given a very powerful vision in which he found himself in vast stadiums all over the world. He said that in each place, the same team was on stage, ministering to the people. He said that in one stadium (which he could tell was somewhere in Asia) he remembers looking over at the rest of the team (which included a band of musicians and singers) and then out at the vast crowd, and he noticed that instead of watching the platform, the people in the stadium were all staring up into the sky. In other words, they were looking to JESUS, rather than to the human vessels that God was using. It is JESUS who must get all the glory. There have been numerous dreams and visions all over the world of stadiums full of people, gathered to hear the gospel and to see and experience the great 'latter rain' outpouring of God's Holy Spirit.

Of course, music will only be one part of this overall picture. There will be incredibly anointed preaching and dramatic healings and miracles that will glorify God in the most profound way also. But the interesting thing about 'music' is the impact that it has, especially amongst the youth. No doubt we are all aware of the tremendous way in which the devil was able to use popular music in the late 1960's to literally "eastern-ise" the thinking and spiritual beliefs of an entire generation (a 'cultural revolution' from which the West has never fully recovered). Isn't God more powerful (and more 'creative'!) than Satan? Therefore, shouldn't true Christian music be the most stunning music that you or I have ever heard? And shouldn't it be used to take territory away from the devil?

I believe that many, many 'new music' ministries are about to arise in true "Revival" power, to glorify God on the streets of every city. In the dreams and visions that James Ryle was given, he was shown that a "new sound" will arise that will sweep the world – a new 'street-level' praise music, mightily anointed of God. I believe that music itself was originally created for the purpose of praising and glorifying Him. So why shouldn't such music be heard in the earth again? I am convinced that the devil's own guns are about to be turned upon him. I believe that the music that is about to arise will help destroy many 'works' that have taken years for him to build. After all, why SHOULD the devil have all the best music? This is part of the devil's territory that will definitely be "taken" in the coming Revival, I believe.

The new music that is about to arise will contain many of the same themes as the other forms of 'Revival' ministry. All the different types of ministry will work together. This new music is to be a Bride's songs of love and praise to her glorious King, and also the sound of an army preparing for war – a kind of "battle" music – raw, powerful, even 'violent' at times. It is to be a 'war cry', calling sinners to repentance and rallying God's people to battle, as well as publicly lifting high the name of our glorious Saviour and Lord. This 'new praise' will not be suited to a comfortable, peace-time church, but rather to a warlike people – a people preparing to "take the kingdom by force". I believe that it will shock a lot of Christians. It will be SO SIMPLE, yet powerful, and above all else it will exalt the name of JESUS CHRIST, our Warrior King. Do not expect this music to be something of mind-blowing complexity. Rather, expect something of an almost child-like simplicity and 'catchiness', but also with real power.

It will not be the slick "professional"-type musicians who will unearth this new sound. No! Many of these lack the necessary humility – too busy seeking technical polish and perfection. Rather, it will be those with a simple heart after Jesus – a great love and a hunger for Him; this is by far the most important factor. It is SPIRITUAL PREPARATION, not musical perfection that God is looking for here. Only those who have died to pride, died to slick "showmanship" and died to the desire to glorify themselves, can ever hope to have a part in this anointing and this 'new sound'. Like other end-time ministries, I believe that God is about to raise up many unknown and 'hidden' Christians into this music area. Truly, "many that are first shall be last, and many that are last shall be first" (Mt 19:30).

HOLINESS AND FAITH

In the coming Reformation and Revival, God is going to deal very deeply with sin, compromise, conformity to the world and materialism amongst His people. As stated earlier, the Scriptures show that Jesus cannot return until a Bride is prepared for Him that is "without spot or wrinkle or any such thing". Today's church is crippled by sin and compromise in the lives of individual Christians (e.g., unforgiveness, gossip, backbiting, "white" lies, pretense, lust, financial dishonesty, worldliness, etc). However, when God really begins to move, the repentance that will occur will go very deep. As Frank Bartleman (a leader in the 1906 'Azusa Street' Revival) stated, "I received from God early in 1905 the following keynote to revival: 'THE DEPTH OF REVIVAL WILL BE DETERMINED EXACTLY BY THE DEPTH OF THE SPIRIT OF REPENTANCE'. And this will obtain for all people, at all times." Anyone who has studied Revival history will acknowledge the obvious truth of this statement. In fact, historically speaking it would be fair to say that DEEP REPENTANCE LIES AT THE HEART OF EVERY TRUE REVIVAL.

Several years ago, a prophet friend of mine was given a whole series of stunning visions of the coming move of God. In several visions, he saw vast numbers of people gathered to hear the most searching, anointed repentance preaching. The conviction of sin amongst the people was just incredible, bringing tremendous 'godly sorrow' and deep repentance. Such scenes have been very common in many great Revivals of the past. And the coming move of God will be no different.

The (almost unheard-of today) experience of "justification by faith" (as the old Revivalists such as Wesley and Finney used to preach it) will also be proclaimed once again in this Revival. Speaking of his own experience, Charles Finney wrote: "In this state I was taught the doctrine of justification by faith as a present experience... I could not feel a sense of guilt or condemnation by any effort I could make. My sense of guilt was gone, my sins were gone, and I do not think I felt any more sense of guilt than if I never had sinned... I felt myself justified by faith, and, so far as I could see, I was in a state in which I did not sin."

It is clear from the Scriptures that the above experience is to be regarded as "normal" for all Christians (see 1 Jn 3, etc). In fact, this will be seen as 'elementary level' Christianity by all who are to be involved in the coming Revival (i.e., walking in a state of having "no knowledge of present sin"). If this seems bizarre to you then please read 'Romans' again! This is totally "normal" stuff. The believers in the coming Revival will walk in a state of total heart-purity before God. Their consciences will be completely clean, and they will WALK in this state by faith. They will not need to strive to maintain it. This will simply be the normal state of their heart before God. This is what walking in true "justification by faith" really means.

Chapter Two

THE LAODICEAN CHURCH

For many years now, numerous prominent Christian leaders have been quite open with their opinion that we live today in the age of the lukewarm or 'Laodicean' church. In the past fifteen years or so, however, this recognition of the church's alarmingly low spiritual state has taken on added urgency, as God has spoken again and again to prophetic ministries around the world, warning that the church is indeed 'Laodicean', and that judgment is about to "begin at the house of God" (1 Pe 4:17). Clearly, a tremendous "shaking" and judgment are about to come upon today's church.

The Laodicean church is the last of the seven churches that Jesus addresses in the book of Revelation (Rev 3:14-22). During this passage, Jesus makes the following "promise" to the lukewarm church: "So then because you are lukewarm, and neither cold nor hot, I WILL SPEW YOU OUT OF MY MOUTH... Be zealous therefore, AND REPENT." It is clear from this passage that the Laodicean church exists under imminent threat of judgment – of being "spewed out" of the mouth of God. The only hope is deep repentance, and that immediately. Please remember that this is a PROMISE of God. It is not an idle threat. Unless there is swift and deep repentance, then God PROMISES to spew the lukewarm church out of His mouth. It is my belief that the role of a prophet is to be a kind of 'watchman on the walls', to loudly warn those who sleep of approaching danger. In the current situation, there can be little doubt that a prophet's job would be to 'sound the alarm in Zion' – to loudly warn the people until they are awakened to the very real danger of imminent judgment. Prophets are never supposed to be 'comfortable' preachers. As A.G. Gardiner said, "When a prophet is accepted and deified, his message is lost. The prophet is only useful so long as he is stoned as a public nuisance calling us to repentance, disturbing our comfortable routines, breaking our respectable idols, shattering our sacred conventions..." I have to say that I have been a little disappointed with some of today's prophets in this regard. It seems to me that a number of them have chosen to emphasize all the 'positive' aspects of the coming harvest, rather than warning of the present imminent danger. Surely, if a prophet is shown that judgment is imminent, then he must use every available means to urgently warn the people? Otherwise he is not fulfilling what God has commissioned him to do, surely?

It is very clear, both prophetically and from the Scriptures, that today's Laodicean church faces imminent and severe judgment, and that the Christians must be warned with great urgency. There is an old saying: "The people will not flee danger until they see it". That is the express purpose of this chapter: seeing the danger. I make no apologies for the directness or the urgency of the message contained herein.

Some people today believe that the 'Toronto blessing' has renewed the church. From my observations, however, the manifestations and experiences associated with Toronto seem to have made little significant impact on the overall 'Laodicean' state of today's church (as I think should become evident from this and later chapters).

Some years ago I made a study of the difference between the New Testament Church as described in the book of Acts, and today's church. I was alarmed to find that in nearly every respect today's Christianity is so different from that of the Bible as to beggar belief. In New Testament times, the Church was like a 'consuming fire' that swept over the whole world, "destroying the works of the devil". Led by fiery, anointed men of God, the early believers constituted a bold, militant, uncompromising force, dedicated to pulling down the devil's strongholds wherever they could be found. These were the 'ground assault' troops of the Most High. They endured much suffering, hardship and persecution in order to see the gospel preached 'in all the earth' in their day.

Today, however, we seemingly prefer to set sail for the kingdom of heaven with a little more "style". We are told in the Bible that in the last days, men will be "lovers of pleasures more than lovers of God". We are also told that, "the time will come when they will not endure sound doctrine; but after their own lusts shall they heap to themselves teachers, having itching ears" (2 Tim 4:3). Isn't it true that we modern believers have invented for ourselves a kind of instant, convenient, 'fast- food' Christianity? A Christianity where all too often the preachers feel it is their role to entertain and cajole, rather than to convict and awaken? A Christianity where for many years now, seeking after 'blessings' has seemingly replaced 'hungering and thirsting' after God? A Christianity that is seemingly more concerned with "happiness" than real holiness? Who could deny that this century finds itself home to what is probably the most comfortable, the most materialistic, the most 'fat' and well-fed church in recorded history?

Jesus reported the cry of the Laodicean church as being: "I am rich and increased with goods, and have NEED OF NOTHING" (Rev 3:17). Incredibly, as we see from this statement, the Laodicean church DOES NOT EVEN RECOGNIZE HER OWN APPALLING SPIRITUAL NAKEDNESS AND BANKRUPTCY. She honestly believes that "all is well"! Certainly, no-one could imagine an era when the church has had so many 'toys', both physical and spiritual. "Rich and increased with goods" we most certainly are in these materialistic days: lavish church buildings, costly radio and TV programs, book shops crammed with every conceivable teaching aid and religious gift, expensive conferences and seminars supplying yet more ear-fattening teaching to those with enough dollars to attend. Who could deny that Christianity is 'big business' these days? Several years ago it was announced in the US that one of the largest Christian music companies was suing another for as much as $20 million in a dispute arising from a distribution agreement.

On an individual level, things are almost as bad. The Bible says, "Love not the world, neither the things that are in the world. If any man love the world, THE LOVE OF THE FATHER IS NOT IN

HIM" (1 Jn 3:15). But who could deny that many Christians today are seemingly more devoted to their 'career' (or to their possessions, or their television) than they are to God? Jesus clearly stated, "You cannot serve God and mammon", yet how many Christians today expend all their energy trying to keep both camps happy? The Bible tells us, "Be not conformed to this world", yet how many Christians today have lifestyles, ambitions and possessions that are literally identical to those of the covetous, materialistic world all around them?

As Jesus Himself stated, "Not everyone who says to me, 'Lord, Lord,' shall enter the kingdom of heaven, but he who does the will of my Father who is in heaven. On that day many will say to me, 'Lord, Lord, did we not prophesy in your name, and cast out demons in your name, and do many mighty works in your name?' And then will I declare to them, 'I NEVER KNEW YOU; DEPART FROM ME, YOU EVILDOERS'" (Mt 7:21-23). "Behold, this was the iniquity of your sister Sodom: pride, fullness of bread, abundance of idleness was in her and in her daughters, neither did she strengthen the hand of the poor and needy..." (Ez 16:49).

Rather than give our money to the poor, today we Christians seemingly prefer to give it to the 'church building fund' or other big, glossy ministries. And while 40,000 children die each day of starvation and disease, and the world goes to hell all around us, we sit comfortably 'at ease in Zion', singing our happy songs about how much we love Jesus and long to be like Him. "Why do you call me Lord, Lord, and do not the things that I say?" is still our grieving Savior's lament. "This people draw nigh to me with their mouth, and honor me with their lips, but their heart is far from me," says the Lord (Mt 15:8). Probably more than any other, this generation of Christians has been guilty of diluting (or betraying) everything that Jesus stood for, and watering down what He said. Little wonder that we have become the laughing-stock of men and of devils. Instead of preaching 'death to self' and 'taking up the cross', today we prefer a more "comfortable" message: "Jesus loves you and has a wonderful plan for your life" (while the music gently plays, of course). A convenient, selfish 'Santa Claus' gospel for a convenience-loving, self-obsessed generation. Is it any wonder that we have a lukewarm church, when the gospel we preach is so lukewarm?

Today the whole of western society is in disarray: Broken marriages, youth suicides, teenage pregnancies, gang violence, drugs, etc, etc. Every year, it seems like the devil is gaining more and more ground, while the influence of today's sickly, "happiness club" church just keeps growing smaller. We are supposed to be the 'salt of the earth', salting the world with Godliness and truth. Surely then, a good portion of the blame for this disastrous mess can be laid directly at the feet of the church? Jesus stated that salt that has lost its savor is "good for nothing, but to be cast out, and to be trodden under foot by men" (Mt 5:13). The world is desperate for answers, but all we have to feed them is insipid, watered-down rubbish. And yet what do we hear today's 'Laodicean' church cry?: "I am rich and increased with goods, and have need of nothing!" Sick, insipid, lukewarm church – how will you escape the judgment that God has promised you?

Today it seems almost as though the church has made some kind of pact with the devil: We won't attack you too hard, if you won't attack us! (I tell you now, the new move of God will have no such treaty!) It makes no sense for the devil to bring real persecution upon today's church: Better to let them sleep! After all, we are certainly not doing him a lot of harm in our present state. How easily ignored is today's church! Almost the only time the world sits up and takes real notice is when there is some big scandal or something else to laugh at. As I said before, we have become the laughing-stock of an entire generation, both of men and of devils.

It is well-known that "music" often accurately represents and depicts the culture it comes from. And it doesn't take too long, when listening to today's Christian radio, to come to the conclusion that if the music is anything to go by, then today's Christianity is in a pretty sick and tepid state. If we were to be brutally honest, we would have to say that very often, our music seems to be little more than 'muzak' – wallpaper music with Christian lyrics; music that wouldn't seem out of place in a lift or a supermarket. But in a supposedly lively, vital Christianity? In my opinion, even the local 'Easy-listening' station seems more musically adventurous than the local Christian station! Even so-called 'contemporary' Christian music often seems to be either a desperately "cool" – or tamed-down – rehash of secular styles from one or two years earlier, again with (vaguely) Christian lyrics over the top. Where is the creativity, the vitality, the life? Why are we musically so far behind the world, if the Creator of the whole Universe is on our side? Why isn't the world following our lead, instead of us following theirs?

It is high time we acknowledged the sorry fact: Today's Christian music is largely embarrassing, predictable and lukewarm. This is simply due to the fact that today's CHRISTIANITY is largely embarrassing, predictable and lukewarm. But such things will not be said of the coming move of God. When true Revival comes, the music will be alive with the creativity and the fire of God, because that is exactly how His people will be.

JUDGEMENT AND REFORMATION

It is significant to note that when the people of Israel fell into a state of serious spiritual decline, God often held the kings and spiritual shepherds of Israel directly responsible for the nation's degenerate state. Often, the judgment that fell upon the leaders at such times was far harsher than that which fell upon the nation as a whole. We see this principle at work right down through the Old and New Testaments. It is interesting to note that Jesus spoke essentially the same message to the religious leaders of His day, as had been spoken to the disobedient king Saul: "The kingdom shall be taken from you and given to another" (1 Sa 28:17 and Mt 21:43). As we shall see, this replacement of one leadership with another – the "kingdom" being taken away from one and given elsewhere – is the very essence of true "Reformation".

Throughout the history of both Israel and the church, every new move of God has involved the raising up of new leaders, with God often bypassing or bringing judgment upon the existing leadership. So it is not surprising that it has frequently been the existing leaders who have persecuted new moves of God the worst (often out of jealousy). And the coming Reformation and Revival will surely be no different.

It is time to face the obvious and brutal truth: It is simply not possible to have a lukewarm church unless the leaders are lukewarm, just as Israel was not able to fall into a state of worldliness or idolatry unless her kings and shepherds were men of compromise. The Bible is very clear that those who are raised up as leaders or teachers amongst God's people will be subject to a much "stricter" judgment (James 3:1). However, I do not believe that God can even afford to have such men leading His church for long. This is why He has been so clearly saying that the coming Revival (like many before it) has been designed to LARGELY BYPASS AND SIDELINE THE CURRENT CHURCH LEADERSHIP. This is not "rebellion". It is simply a statement of obvious truth, backed by the history of Revival and Reformation right down through the ages. God has been forced to take such drastic action many times in the past, and this Revival will be no exception.

Like Israel, many of today's church leaders have clearly been guilty of compromising (diluting or toning down) God's word to His people over many years. They have surrendered, in varying degrees, to the 'fear of man'. Many of them are afraid to preach uncompromising truth to their congregations for fear that some of the people will become "offended" (not forgetting who pays their salary!). Instead, in their preaching, it almost seems as if they have adopted the modern marketing creed: "Accentuate the positive and eliminate the negative" (complete with jokes and amusing anecdotes, of course). No 'sin, righteousness and judgment' preaching here! And, of course, no desperately needed REPENTANCE for the lukewarm church, either.

As history shows, God must very often have entirely new leaders and a new movement to go with His new outpouring. This is what true "Reformation" has always been about. And sadly, whenever God is about to do something completely new, many leaders, feeling threatened, oppose it with every ounce of their being. This has unfortunately always been the way.

As Frank Bartleman noted, "A revival almost always begins amongst the laity. The ecclesiastical leaders seldom welcome reformation. History repeats itself..." And indeed, the history of the church is full of instances of respected Christian leaders persecuting the 'new move' of God. As has often been the case, today's preachers are largely way too comfortable with the status quo. They have their cozy organizations and their church machinery, their governing bodies and their 'keep the people happy' routines. And God is about to "SHAKE" it all to such a degree that much of it will be literally 'shaken to pieces'.

What God really needs in times of Revival are bold and anointed 'Joshuas', who will urge the people onward to "possess the land" – to 'take the kingdom by force'. For God's people in these last days are to be a people of war, and they must be led by men of war. And this is exactly the kind of leadership that He is about to raise up, to lead His people on in the coming great Revival.

SOULISHNESS IN THE CHURCH

For the past twenty years or so, I have had first-hand involvement with the Charismatic/Pentecostal movement. And I have to say that it has greatly saddened me over that time, to watch the gradual decline of this movement into what I felt was an ever more shallow, 'feelings, emotions and experiences'-based Christianity. The preaching seemed to become ever-more laden with warm 'positive-speak' and hype, the music became ever-more slick and entertaining, and the people seemed to be more and more interested in 'having a good time', seeking a blessing, or seeking an emotional 'touch from the Lord', rather than seeking God for His own sake. The preachers and worship leaders obviously began to feel that they had to 'entertain' the people to keep them attending, and the people began to EXPECT to be entertained.

What this actually represents is a huge swing away from 'Holy Spirit-based' Christianity to a Christianity that is based in the "soul" area of man. As is well-known, the soul is the seat of man's feelings and emotions, etc. What makes 'soulish' Christianity so dangerous is that mere feelings and emotions (which can come through just playing the right kind of music, or from any number of sources) begin to play a more and more pivotal role in the walk of the believer. He or she begins to rely on the weekly church service to get that emotional 'lift'. A Christianity that starts to revolve around such feelings and experiences is wide open to deception (as history demonstrates again and again). The soul area of man is notorious for its ability to be manipulated. Any movement that cultivates "soulish" experiences is simply opening its people up to what could easily become demonic delusion. This is why the Bible exhorts us to 'be not carnally minded', and speaks of 'death to self', etc. The fallen soul area is the area that most needs to be 'crucified' in us.

This is not to say that we should become joy-less or 'emotionless' by any means! But what it does mean is that we need to be able to recognize and avoid soulish manipulation or false 'spiritual' experiences of this kind. We must seek to worship God 'in spirit and in truth', rather than with this kind of soulish excess. For where there is 'soul-power' operating, the devil will always get involved. Some of the most well-known cults, pagan religions, and New Age therapies, etc, revolve around soulish experiences that open people up to demonic forces. And as is well known, soul-power is also at the heart of witchcraft. This is real 'Jezebel' territory.

An intercessor that I know was given a very significant dream which relates directly to this subject. In it, she found herself in the "control room" of a large Pentecostal church. She was there because she was to lead the worship in the church that week, and she had already chosen the songs she felt were to be used.

However, there was a woman in the control room – a rather 'brazen', painted, sensuously-dressed woman (Jezebel) – who acted as if she was in charge, and began to go through the songs, replacing many of them with her own choices. The intercessor then discovered that the songs this woman had chosen were very 'sensuous', off-color, worldly songs! And this was supposed to be for the worship service! With righteous anger, she said to the woman, "This place is full of the spirit of Jezebel, and you're more full of it than anyone!" The woman then sobbed pathetically (not out of repentance, but rather because she had been exposed – 'Jezebel' will often react in this way). When the intercessor asked the name of the pastor of the church, she was told that he was called 'Pastor Greymouth'.

She believes that what God was showing her in this dream was that the strongman of 'Compromise' which is dominating much of today's leadership is allowing Jezebel to bring her sensuous, controlling influence into the church, and this is seen particularly in the worship. (Remembering that 'sensuous' means "appealing to the senses").

Along with the rise of 'soulishness' in the church over the past twenty years or more, have come a whole raft of new methods and techniques for keeping the people "happy and involved" with the church. It seems like hardly a year has gone by without the arrival of some 'new, improved' church growth technique or youth program. After all, the people must be kept "entertained", mustn't they? The church has been loaded down with man-made activities, methods and seminars, all organized, funded and run according to the "brilliant ideas" of men, and yet claiming the blessing of God's hand. Let's be honest here, very little of this has been God's idea at all. Like almost everything in the church today, much of it has been essentially man-pleasing, man-centered and man-entertaining.

In a very real way, today's blind, "Laodicean" church could well be likened to a crippled, cancer-ridden woman who has learnt how to apply clothes and make-up in such a way as to disguise her terrible condition, and has convinced herself that if she keeps up the "blessings", keeps herself active and puts on a good outward 'show', then all will be well. "I am rich and increased with goods, and have need of nothing," is her cry, but much of her 'happy' organizing feels ominously like 'rearranging deck chairs on the Titanic' to me. Like the Emperor with his new clothes, it matters little how active we are, or how much "noise" we make, the fact is today's church is, in reality, utterly spiritually naked. And only when the great 'shaking' and Reformation come, will the full extent of this nakedness be revealed.

As stated previously, the Laodicean church will clearly have no part in the coming move of God. Rather, as has occurred many times down through history, God is going to bring a cleansed and purified "remnant" out from the current church system, 'tried as by fire', to help gather in the great end-times harvest. Before this great Revival truly begins, however, I believe that the Laodicean church will be given one last chance to repent. God will raise up ministries and 'voices' to call the lukewarm church to her knees, and then out onto the streets. I believe that many will heed this call and will repent before it is too late. God will bring them out onto the streets, to become part of the great "Street-Revival" that is about to explode around the world. In many ways, it could be said that the coming 'harvest' will first begin within the church. This has always been the way. True Revival has always been aimed firstly at "reviving" God's wayward people, and then sending them out with great power to display His grace and glory to a dying world. And so, repentance must first begin with the Christians.

However, there will also be many who will refuse to heed this 'repentance' message, thereby placing themselves in severe danger of imminent judgment. It surely cannot be long before all that God has promised is fulfilled, and judgment truly "begins at the house of God". In fact, it is my belief that this time is now very near. The storm-clouds are gathered, and a great 'dividing' or polarization is about to occur in the church. No-one will be able to sit on the fence. They will have to choose whether to cling to Laodicea, or throw in their lot with the 'violent', controversial, new "upstart" preachers. Such has always been the choice facing God's people in times of Revival. However, because we are in the 'last days', I believe that this time the two groups will be even more clearly distinguished and separated than usual, just like 'tares and wheat' (Mt 13). One group will go on to great blessing, and the other to certain judgment. I do not believe that God can live with a Laodicean church. And all over the world, God has been saying that this judgment is now 'imminent', even at the doors. The tremendous "SHAKING" of the church is about to begin.

Chapter Three

RELIGIOUS EXTREMES: LEGALISM VS. LICENSE

Human beings are unfortunately creatures of extremes, and the devil has used this many, many times over the centuries to bind and deceive the church. If he cannot push us too far one way, then he will try to push us as far as he can in the opposite direction. There are many different forms of bondage and deception that the church has succumbed to over the years. Two of the most prevalent of these have been in the area of "religious" extremes: Pharisee-style legalism and spiritual pride on the one hand, and "hyper-grace", the casting off of restraint, and 'experience-centered' Christianity on the other.

Over the past ten years or so, there has been a tremendous amount of teaching exposing the "legalism" side of religion, and this has been a very good thing. However, not surprisingly, the pendulum seems to have now swung right over to the opposite extreme, particularly in many Pentecostal/Charismatic churches, and we are now seeing what I believe is an equally dangerous over-emphasis: Hyper-liberty or 'hyper-grace' teaching, which can also lead to great error (as it has done many times down through history).

The purpose of this chapter is to expose in detail the often-subtle (yet deadly) snares of the devil at both extremes of this religious spectrum. It is interesting to note that both extremes are largely just a distortion of good, solid Christian truths. The 'legalism/ condemnation' extreme is often just a harsh distortion of true repentance/ holiness teaching, while the 'hyper- grace' extreme is largely a distortion of true teaching on the liberty that we have in Christ, etc. What happens is that these genuine truths are pushed to extremes through over-emphasis, and they end up becoming so unbalanced that they in fact become dangerous error. Even though the 'hyper-grace' extreme is the one that I believe is currently predominant in many churches, I do want to take a detailed look at both extremes, beginning with the "legalism" side.

The most well-known proponents of this 'legalistic' form of religion were, of course, the scribes and Pharisees of Jesus' time. Many people think that the legalism of the Pharisees largely just revolved around 'tradition', but there was far more to it than that. Religion of this kind is often very subtle, taking on a large variety of shapes and forms. Jesus spoke of it as being like 'leaven', which spreads like a cancer until everything it touches is affected. I think that many Christians would be very surprised at the degree to which Pharisee-type religion has been present in the modern church, in one form or another. It is truly deadly stuff! This section is designed to expose many of these aspects of legalistic religion that have so influenced the church in modern times.

Without a doubt, one of the most obvious elements of pharisaic religion is "conservatism" (a love of the old ways, and a resistance to anything new). It is apparent that there are still many Christians (though far less than there used to be) who have still not come to terms with the 1960's, let alone the 1990's. Their Christianity is still greatly oriented towards a "respectable, middle class, conservative" approach to life, and they tend to judge people (particularly the youth) by whether or not their hairstyles, their clothes, or their music styles, etc, conform to their own rather drab, conservative standards. In other words, they are tremendously prone to judging people by their 'outward appearance' rather than by the 'heart'. To them, these outward factors are issues of the utmost importance.

What impression do worldly people get when they enter the churches of such Christians? (Remembering that these visitors may well be gang members, drug addicts, New Agers, etc). All too often, I believe that the impression they get is that the only type of people God really likes are the sugary-"nice", neatly dressed, clean-cut, respectable kind. They get the feeling that they would first of all have to change the way they dress, the way they express themselves, their hairstyle, their whole way of doing things, before they could ever come and be truly accepted by God. Because, as everyone knows, God only likes "nice, respectable" people, doesn't He?

And tell me, what is the unspoken message that some church leaders are still sending out today? Isn't it that you must be slick, well-dressed and (usually) Bible-college trained if you want to minister in front of others? These are just some of the lies that still influence many peoples' view of Christianity. And very often they have been passed on without us even opening our mouths! Many worldly people still see Bible-believing Christianity as being dreary, conservative and backward-looking (either that, or rather "weird"). It just doesn't seem 'relevant' to them at all. I tell you now that such unspoken messages are going to change in the coming Revival. In fact, in many ways they will be the exact opposite of what they have been. What people are really looking for is a relevant, down to earth, yet miraculous and Spirit-filled Christianity. This is what the early Church had, and this is exactly what the coming move of God will bring in also.

It is very clear from the Scriptures that Jesus deliberately identified Himself with the poor and the "sinners" during His time on earth. Both He and His message were extremely 'relevant' to the street-level people of His time. Born in a filthy stable, He also chose to die the death of a common criminal, strung up between two thieves on a wooden cross. The Pharisees bitterly criticized Him during His ministry for His apparent 'laxness' in enforcing the religious codes of conduct on His followers. Jesus didn't seem strict enough or outwardly "holy" enough for them! He didn't look right, He didn't dress right, and He didn't sound right, and His disciples were even worse! What a motley low-life bunch they must have seemed to the cultured, educated religious leaders of their day! After all, "Can any good thing come out of Nazareth?"

The Pharisees spoke scathingly of Jesus as being a "friend of sinners". But Jesus didn't mind. He had come to 'seek and save that which was lost'. He said, "John came neither eating nor drinking, and they say, 'He has a demon'; the Son of Man came eating AND DRINKING, and they say, 'Behold, a glutton and a drunkard, a friend of tax-collectors and sinners!' Yet wisdom is justified by her deeds" (Mt 11:18-19). Jesus was a friend of the common people. He spent most of His time with them, sharing both their joys and their sorrows. He understood them and spoke their language. It was the religious types who persecuted Him the most. Eventually they crucified Him.

Like many Revivals, I believe that the coming one will meet the same kind of response as always from the religious and the judgmental. John Wesley was scathingly denounced in his day: "... He and his lay-lubbers – his ragged legion of preaching tinkers, scavengers, draymen and chimney sweepers, etc. – go forth to poison the minds of men." Wesley's policy was much the same as that of the Salvation Army: "... go always not only to those who need you, but to those who need you most." His was also a 'street movement' in every sense of the term. And it was Wesley (along with Martin Luther and William Booth) who was quoted as saying, "Why should the devil have all the best music?" These men wanted a Christianity that was vital and relevant to the street-level people of their day. That is why they used the 'pub' music of their time for their praise and battle hymns!

To me, one sign that someone may have a legalistic 'religious' stronghold in their life is that they cannot see how God could possibly use today's Rock music in any way. In fact, these people are no different to the religionists who opposed the early Salvation Army's music on exactly the same grounds. What they are often guilty of is judging this style of music by its 'outward appearance', rather than seeing how the changed 'heart' of it could be greatly used to glorify God. In actual fact, I cannot think of a better form of music to use for 'battle-hymns' myself!

KEEPING UP APPEARANCES

It is still true of much of Christendom today that "keeping up appearances" has become an integral part of many believers' lives. All too often, new converts seem to get the impression that the first thing they need to learn about the Christian walk is how to look and act "the part" in front of others. They seem to conclude that it is the 'outward' things that really matter. And so, to fit in, they begin to unconsciously obey our unspoken list of modern Christian do's and don'ts: Thou shalt smile and look 'loving' at every opportunity in church, thou shalt raise your hands and clap with everyone else (lest they think that something is 'wrong' with you), thou shalt not say "crap" or pick thy nose, thou shalt look and act like a "good Christian" at all times. What are we passing on to these new converts? Very simply, we are establishing within them what has, in many cases, become one of the great foundations of modern Christianity: 'PRETENSE' (i.e., How to put on a good 'outward show').

In the Bible, pretense was known by another name: "HYPOCRISY". Jesus said, "Woe unto you, scribes and Pharisees, hypocrites! For you are like white-washed graves, which indeed appear beautiful on the outside, but within are full of dead men's bones and all uncleanness" (Mt 23:27). It is still true today that many of our churches are quite literally packed with "great pretenders" – people who know how to dress nicely, to smile warmly and say 'bless you', to seem outwardly like real, 'spiritually together' Christians – yet who have little deep relationship with God at all. The church has been like this for years. Surely this is nothing less than Pharisee-style hypocrisy wrapped in a modern cloak?

In much of modern Christendom, this kind of pretense is still considered to be "normal". Many believers have been pretending to be "good Christians" for so long now that they have actually come to believe their own lie! Whenever they are around other Christians, they suddenly become unbearably "nice", joyful and 'loving'. This is not true, 'Holy Spirit' love at all, but rather an out-

and-out, self-manufactured forgery. I call this 'pseudo' or false love. It has nothing to do with the fruit of the Holy Spirit. It is totally manufactured. And who could deny that this kind of pretense is right through today's church? I am convinced that false love, false humility, and false spirituality are still rampant throughout Christendom today. Having to be "seen" to do and say all the right things, etc, is still one of the great strongholds of Pharisee-type religion affecting modern Christians.

I am convinced that what God really wants is a people who, rather than being "great pretenders", are actually one hundred percent 'real' in every way (i.e., no pretense at all). In fact, I believe that God wants us to be truly transparent; not only in our words, but also in the way we act around others. We are to be "real", down-to-earth people in a world that is crying out for reality and truth. Putting on a false 'Christian' front is actually just another form of dishonesty or lying.

The idea that 'walking in love' involves being unbearably "nice" to everybody all the time is also, I believe, one of the most harmful and false things about modern Christianity. Because this kind of "love" is so desperate not to offend anyone, it often ends up compromising the truth just to keep people happy. In 1 Cor 13:6 we are told that true Holy Spirit love "does not rejoice with iniquity, but rejoices with the truth". This is a good test. Very often, today's Christians are afraid to strongly challenge sin or lukewarmness in the church, because to do so would be "unloving". And so they compromise the truth by staying silent when they should be speaking out. The fact is this is not true "love" at all. It is compromise! True 'Holy Spirit' love will always care enough to speak vital truth, even if some people may be offended by it. After all, it is better to risk offending others, than to risk them going to hell. We see this principle at work many times in Jesus' own ministry.

You can be sure that those whom God is going to use in the coming Revival will be extremely "real", down-to-earth type people. They will also be absolutely fearless in 'speaking the truth in love' without compromise, no matter what the cost. They will be tremendously misunderstood and persecuted at times, but will literally "love not their lives unto the death". This will be God's holy army – a glorious, spotless Bride, totally befitting a Husband who is the King of all kings and the Lord of all lords. As I have said before, many of these cleansed and anointed 'Bridal' warriors will seem quite rough and 'unsuitable' to many people from the outside, but to God it is the "inside" that counts (remembering that some of His greatest apostles were rather 'rough' ex-fishermen, etc). On the inside, these men and women will have been washed "whiter than snow", and they will walk with total transparency and heart purity before God. Their one desire will be to love and glorify Him with all their 'heart, mind, soul and strength'. And they will go forth with great power, "destroying the works of the devil" in His name.

THE DAM BURSTS

Some time ago, an intercessor sent me a copy of a vision that she had had, in which a huge dam that was holding back a vast quantity of water, crumbled from the top downwards, layer by layer, thereby releasing a great flood of water. God had shown her that the dam in the vision was "man's structure", which was holding back His appointed ministries (and His anointing) from flooding out over the nation. At the appointed time, this structure will be unable to hold back the 'bursting forth' of ministries that God has ordained for the last days. These will be ministries that have been in hidden preparation for years, awaiting God's time.

Who could deny that today's church structures do indeed seem almost purpose-designed to largely thwart God's purposes for His people? In fact, I would go as far as to say that the devil himself could hardly have thought up a better way of keeping the church bound and in chains, than our present church structures and set-up! Essentially, what we still have today is a "priesthood/laity" system, in which a small number of men are sent off to Bible College to gain knowledge, degrees and diplomas, and are then appointed to be the professional, "qualified" leaders of church congregations. This is totally unscriptural. In fact, it would be very doubtful whether many of the original apostles would have even been able to pass today's entrance exams, let alone gain a full 'degree in divinity' or diploma of theology!

The "priesthood/laity" system was greatly used of the devil to keep the Catholic Church in bondage for centuries. As soon as you have one man, or a small group of men appointed as "professionals" to run everything, then much of the simplicity and the vitality of primitive Christianity is lost. The church itself (not the "accredited" Bible-college system) is supposed to be a perpetual breeding ground for new, anointed ministries to be continuously rising up, "full of faith and of the Holy Spirit". (See for example, the cases of Philip and Stephen, in the book of Acts). In today's church, however, the "qualified professionals" tend to run around doing everything (for this is what they're paid to do, after all!) while the congregation sit and watch. Anyone who is likely to bring a truly convicting or 'uncomfortable' message is not welcome to speak because the leadership have a vested interest in keeping everything "running" smoothly. The people must be kept 'happy' after all (lest they go someplace else)!

What we have today is really a whole bunch of "happiness clubs" rather than real churches. The people pay their 'fees' and sit back while the "professionals" do the work. We have ruined the church by turning her into something that she was never meant to be: an 'institution'. And institutions almost always feel threatened by large-scale change or Reformation. It is very clear from what God has been saying that He has no desire to merely "revamp" today's church structures. They are well past that kind of remedy. He cannot afford to have the new Revival ruined by being crammed into the old, suffocating 'boxes'. Rather, He is simply going to "spew" these structures out of His mouth (along with all who choose to cling to them). This is not an idle threat. In fact, as I have already said, I believe that this great "shaking" is very near now.

THE MANY GUISES OF "PHARISEE-TYPE" RELIGION

So far in our discussion of this 'legalistic' religious extreme, we have spoken about conservatism, 'keeping up appearances', and also some of the evils of the present religious structures and systems, etc. The following is a list of some of the other major strongholds of Pharisee-type religion that have greatly affected the church in modern times:

1. SPIRITUAL PRIDE. This is the "biggie" from which many others spring. Basically, spiritual pride is an attitude of self-satisfaction, based on the fact that we do all the "right" things, or believe the "right" doctrines, or belong to the "right" church or stream, etc. It is the opposite of being 'poor in spirit' (i.e., recognizing one's own spiritual poverty). And it often tends to look down rather smugly upon others who don't seem as outwardly 'spiritual' or correct, or perhaps don't belong to the same 'group' as we do.

2. JUDGEMENTALISM. Closely related to spiritual pride, this basically involves judging people by outward appearances, rather than discerning the 'heart'. The Scriptures tell us that "man looks on the outward appearance, but the Lord looks on the heart" (1 Sam 16:7). This is a very important point to grasp. Jesus said, "Judge not, that you be not judged" (Mt 7:1). Judgmental people often harshly 'categorize' people by the way they look or the 'group' they belong to, etc, rather than whether or not they have a real heart after God. There is often little 'mercy' in their attitude. They also tend to "strain at gnats" (judging others over small, trivial points of law, etc).

3. LEGALISM. This involves imposing rules, laws, or "dos and don'ts" upon oneself or others (even unconsciously) from the 'outside'. (True change occurs when the Holy Spirit transforms people from within). Legalism concentrates on correcting outward things by making little "laws" against them, but this has no value whatsoever in God's eyes (for He is concerned about purifying

men's "hearts" first and foremost). Legalism can be strict and condemning. It often involves using the Scriptures as a kind of 'rule-book' (which is an Old Testament approach). The New Testament advocates 'heart purity' and being 'led by the Spirit' instead.

Two examples of Old Testament laws that are often imposed today are Tithing and Sabbath-keeping. However, the New Testament is very clear: "If you are led by the Spirit, you are not under the law" (Gal 5:18. See also Col 2:14-17, Rom 8:1-16, etc). This is why I believe that many of today's Morals Campaigners and Christian Politicians are actually achieving very little for God's kingdom at all. They are seeking to pass laws that may change people outwardly, but will never cleanse their hearts.

4. KNOWLEDGE. This is often a great source of spiritual pride. Those who have gained extensive knowledge of the Bible or of certain doctrines or teachings can tend to look down upon others who don't have the same 'understanding' as themselves. They seem to forget that Jesus chose most of His disciples from amongst the poor and uneducated members of society. It was the Pharisees who were famed for their study and technical knowledge of the Scriptures, and their arguments over quite trivial doctrines and theories, etc.

There is nothing wrong with reading and seeking to understand the Bible, but it is important to remember that it is not just by study or reasoning that we discover the hidden truths of God, but by revelation from the Holy Spirit (1 Cor 2:4-16). Remember, the Pharisees killed the very Messiah that they had been theorizing and studying about for years! (See Jn 5:39-47). "Knowledge puffs up, but love edifies" (1 Cor 8:1). Spiritual knowledge of any kind has the potential to puff us up with pride, and this can be very subtle. Those who have received great revelation, etc, from God are likewise in great danger and must beware of pride creeping in. Secretly regarding oneself as a kind of 'spiritual expert' in any area can be extremely dangerous. And judging people primarily by what is in their 'head' rather than their heart is still wide-spread in modern Christianity.

5. LOVING THE "CHIEF SEATS". Jesus said of the Pharisees that they "loved the chief seats in the synagogues", etc. They loved to be 'seen' to be persons of real spiritual importance. This was a source of great pride to them. (They also loved to be "seen" praying long, 'holy' prayers and giving money to the poor, etc. These things are not wrong in themselves, but it is the MOTIVES behind them that are important). Many Christians even today love to put on a "holy, loving and humble" act in front of others. There are also many who love to be 'seen' associating with the "famous visiting speaker" or sitting on special chairs on the platform, etc. Again, MOTIVES are the important thing here.

6. FLESHLY STRIVING. This is a very common one, especially for the more active or 'zealous' Christians or leaders. I am speaking here of the kind of people who are always busy "doing" things for God, and who often look down on others who don't seem quite as 'devoted' as they are. They are often working very hard for one particular Christian organization, striving to "make the vision happen". They honestly believe that they are 'pleasing God' through all their efforts, their activities, their zeal and their good works, etc.

In actual fact, large numbers of these Christians are serving 'Religion' rather than God. Jesus said that the Pharisees would "compass land and sea" to make one convert. THEY were 'busy for God' as well! There is no "rest" in this kind of striving. People who are caught up in it often feel guilty if they are not "out there, doing something for God". This can eventually lead to total burn-out. Jesus clearly told His disciples to wait until they were "endued with power from on high" before they went out to evangelize. But those who are into striving cannot bear to 'wait'. And thus they end up serving "Religion" instead of God. The religious striving that I am speaking of here is anything that works hard to please God using man's own methods, efforts or abilities.

7. ASCETICISM. This can be a particularly dangerous religious deception. It basically revolves around the idea that we can make ourselves more "holy" simply by denying our body of food, rest, etc. Again, it is an 'outwardly-centered' doctrine. It focuses attention on bodily self-denial rather than on true "holiness and purity of heart". And again it is a distortion of true Biblical practice (genuine Spirit-led fasting, etc). Those who have fallen under this delusion often believe that if they can bring their body under more and more 'subjection' through fasting, suffering and other forms of self-denial, then they will be able to conquer their base desires and become more "pure". This is actually no different to what many Hindu gurus teach, and in its extreme form it will open a Christian up to real demonic bondage and deception.

Self-control is a good thing, but even extremes of "keeping one's body under" can never truly bring about 'death' to our fallen desires. These desires actually have their roots deep within our hearts and souls, not merely in our physical bodies. If we wish to truly deal with them, then we must use SPIRITUAL weapons, rather than mere bodily self-denial (for this will actually achieve little, long-term). As the apostle Paul said, "Why do you submit to regulations, 'Do not handle, Do not taste, Do not touch'...? These have indeed an appearance of wisdom in promoting rigor of devotion and self-abasement and severity to the body, but they are of no value in checking the indulgence of the flesh" (Col 2:20-23). We will discuss the use of true, effective "SPIRITUAL" weapons in dealing with our fallen desires and other 'strongholds' in our lives, at the end of this chapter.

8. CONDEMNATION. This is a feeling of heaviness or despair, a feeling of "never being good enough" to meet God's high expectations. It is very different from being 'convicted' of specific sins by the Holy Spirit, which leads to godly sorrow and repentance. Condemnation occurs when we come under "law", and begin to concentrate on the outward things that we do, rather than on the state of our heart before God. It can sometimes be caused by "heavy" preaching on sin, holiness, etc, that does not carry the anointing of the Holy Spirit. Such preaching brings only spiritual

'death': "The letter kills but the Spirit gives life" (2 Cor 3:6). The working of the Holy Spirit is required to truly expose men's hearts and bring to light any sin in their lives.

Although it is a well-known fact that almost all of the best-known Revivalists used to deliberately preach searching, convicting sermons on "sin, righteousness and judgment", it must also be remembered that these men always preached under the mighty anointing of the Holy Spirit. It was not uncommon for them to preach with tears streaming down their faces. On one occasion, Charles Finney said: "...it seemed to myself as if I could rain hail and love upon them at the same time; or in other words, that I could rain upon them hail in love... I felt like rebuking them with all my heart and yet with a compassion which they could not mistake. I never knew that they accused me of severity, although I think I never spoke with more severity in my life."

I have come across a number of Christians who seem to be experts at bringing condemnation into people's lives. They quite often have the "severity" of Charles Finney, yet entirely lack the genuine 'Revival' anointing that is absolutely essential for this kind of ministry. Such Christians are also often greatly lacking in the 'fruit of the Spirit' (love, joy, peace, etc), both in their preaching and in their own personal lives. Over a period of time, they will bring heaviness, condemnation and domination into the lives of others (rather than deep repentance, liberty and joy). Such people will invariably have huge 'Religious' strongholds in their lives, which must be completely smashed if they are ever to be truly used of God.

9. DOMINATION AND CONTROL. There are still groups around with heavy, controlling leaders, who expect unthinking 'submission' from their flock. True, godly leaders, who walk under His anointing, do not need to use such tactics to maintain their authority. They rely on God to show His approval of their words and ministry. There are still Pastors around today who have used charm, natural ability, charisma, personality (in other words, "soul power") and sometimes even control and manipulation to gain

them prestige and power over others. Until recently, such men often employed the heavy "Covering/Submission" doctrine (which taught that all Christians have to be in abject 'submission' to their Pastor – no matter what) to maintain control of the flock. This doctrine has since been widely recognized as an extremely dangerous 'twisting' of true Scriptural teaching. (In fact, it has been so thoroughly refuted in the past ten years or so that there now seems to be a massive swing over to the other extreme, leaving a 'vacuum' of true, godly authority in the church – the kind of vacuum that the devil loves to exploit; more on this later).

No doubt there are still numerous churches today with relatively 'heavy', dominating, legalistic leaders. However, the number of these has certainly declined greatly over the past ten years or so. This heavy 'submission' doctrine definitely helped perpetuate the current "Priesthood/Laity" system (which in essence, divides Christians irrevocably into two 'classes'). Today, there are other forces at work, reinforcing and exploiting this 'class' system in different ways, but the result always ensures one thing: that the church remains bound in darkness and defeat (and yet is convinced that she is walking in abundant freedom and 'light'!)

10. SECTARIANISM. This is a kind of strong devotion or attachment to one's own group, 'stream' or denomination, rather than to the body of Christ as a whole. 'Sectarian' people often tend to look down on those who are not "one of them". They often firmly believe that THEIR church or THEIR stream is somehow the best, and they love to highlight the (often trivial) differences between their particular group and all the others. Some of them even delight in mocking the others behind their backs, or 'baiting' or provoking them with doctrinal questions, etc. (Actually, an enjoyment of such religious debates is an almost sure sign of the presence of a sizable religious 'stronghold' in a person's life. This is what the Bible is warning of when it speaks of those who are 'contentious' or given to strife, etc).

Christendom today is still full of people who are busy building and promoting their own group or leader at the expense of all the others. What they are doing, in fact, is promoting DIVISION in the Body of Christ. When they do this, these people are not primarily serving GOD'S kingdom at all, but rather whatever 'human' kingdom they have aligned themselves with. And all of these kingdoms carry a different "label". As I have said before, God is going to bring about true unity in the coming Revival by bringing His people out from under all these 'labels' and divisions.

11. ENVY. It is interesting to note that the Bible says that the Chief Priests delivered Jesus up to be killed because of their "envy" of Him (Mk 15:10, etc). What an incredibly subtle yet destructive evil such 'envy' is! The Chief Priests and religious leaders of Jesus' time were obviously envious of His fame, His anointing and authority, and His influence amongst the people. And it was largely from this motive that they schemed and plotted for months to try to discredit or destroy Him. This was the REAL reason behind much of their slander and opposition to His ministry (though it is doubtful that they even realized that this was their true motivation). Envy is very difficult to discern, even within one's own heart. Deadly stuff! And this will be the REAL reason behind much of the opposition to the coming Revival, also.

Anyone who is truly anointed and given influence or authority by God can often expect slander and persecution from others. This has always been the way. Often, the most bitter opposition will come from men who were desiring to be greatly used of God themselves, thus proving that the real motive behind their desire was essentially "selfish ambition", rather than an overwhelming passion to see God glorified. Often such men will also find themselves secretly pleased to hear of the demise or fall of some prominent ministry that they were secretly envious of. How sick and depraved the human heart can be! We must all beware of these kinds of motives operating in our own hearts and lives.

12. TRADITION. We have already touched on a number of the "traditions of men" associated with today's church: The importance placed on degrees and diplomas from Bible college, the 'priesthood/laity' system, our often lavish church buildings (which

are really just modern "cathedrals"), not to mention our many harmful traditions in music, evangelism and preaching, etc. Jesus said of the scribes and Pharisees that "in vain do they worship me, teaching for doctrines the commandments of men" (Mk 7:7).

Just think for a moment, how much of a 'routine' even we Pentecostal/Charismatic Christians have developed over the years. We still all dress up and go to our "Cathedral" once or twice a week, where we sit down, then stand up to sing our "five fast songs followed by five slow songs" (either clapping or raising our hands, depending on the type of song). After about the third 'slow' song, there will usually be a hush for a while (sometimes with 'singing in the Spirit', which will have been completely rehearsed by the musicians). We then sit down for the sermon, after which there is a 'ministry' time, we stand up for a few more songs, place our money in the offering bag, listen to the notices and go home. Week-in and week-out, it is almost always the same. Real "Early church" material! (I think not). And we dare to call the other churches 'traditional'?

One very obvious tradition that has had a central place in Christendom over many centuries (though not in the beginning) is the fact that our church life so greatly revolves around one particular day of the week (usually Sunday). This may seem like a minor point to some, but many of the errors of today's church system have direct links with the whole concept of a "Sabbath-based" Christianity. A number of the early Pentecostal Revivalists also recognized this. Frank Bartleman wrote: "...we drift back continually into the old, backslidden, ecclesiastical conceptions, forms and ceremonies. Thus history sadly ever repeats itself. Now we must work up an annual revival. We go to church on Sundays, etc, etc, just 'like the nations (churches) round about us.' But in the beginning it was not so."

In the book of Acts, the Jerusalem believers gathered DAILY in the huge, open-air temple courtyard. I believe that in the coming Revival, God is going to bring His people right away from "Sunday-based" Christianity, and it will be vital that we stay away.

Otherwise the new move of God will very quickly become just another 'denomination', competing just as all the others do today – holding their meetings all at about the same time each week, so that the Christians are forced to choose which "division" or which "label" they will join. It was the famous Christian writer John Bunyan who declared: "Since you desire to know by what name I wish to be called, I desire, if God should count me worthy, to be called a Christian, a believer, or any other name sanctioned by the Holy Ghost. But as for those factious titles, such as Anabaptists, etc, I believe they came neither from Jerusalem nor Antioch, but rather from hell and Babylon, for they naturally tend to divisions, and ye may know them by their fruits."

As we have seen, those in the church today who find themselves at the "legalistic" end of the religious scale often tend, like the Pharisees, to be the more 'active' or zealous believers. It is very easy for such people to begin to place their "trust" in the fact that they belong to the right church or movement, or that they are so zealous in performing their 'Christian duties': going to meetings, organizing church activities, witnessing, tithing, etc. Even the fact that they read their Bibles more regularly than others can be a source of subtle (yet deadly) spiritual pride. They often tend to look down on those who don't seem as outwardly "devoted" as they are.

Much of this legalistic form of religion involves 'good' things done from wrong motives. Many of these people are unconsciously trying to "work" or use their own efforts to become more pleasing to God, rather than relying solely on the cleansing blood of Christ. In their hearts there is secret pride and judgmentalism, because they feel that their outward 'efforts and duties' make them somehow "better Christians" than the others. This is truly the 'leaven of the Pharisees' in all its deadly subtlety.

OPPOSITE RELIGIOUS EXTREMES

As we have seen, the results of legalistic or "Pharisee-type" religion are: condemnation, heaviness, domination, striving, men-pleasing, etc. This kind of religion is tremendously concerned with outward or 'external' Christian activity. It twists and distorts people's motivation for doing genuinely 'good' things like reading their Bible, seeking true holiness, fasting, etc. And it results in a very harsh, unbalanced Christianity. When the Holy Spirit is truly moving, the balanced, Scriptural Christianity that results is one of genuine conviction of sin, godly sorrow, deep repentance, release, liberty, joy, love, true holiness, etc. This is the Christianity of the New Testament, and also of the coming move of God. Legalism will certainly have no place in the coming Revival. But neither will the opposite religious extreme – 'hyper-grace', hyper-liberty or the "casting off of restraint".

As stated earlier, it seems to me that over the past ten years or so, due to the fact that the dangers of 'legalism' have been recognized more and more by the churches, the pendulum has swung right over to the other extreme. As I said, if the devil cannot push us too far one way, then he will often try to push as far as he can in the opposite direction. There are demonic spirits behind both of these extremes. (Probably both ends use largely the same spirits. I doubt whether they mind which end we Christians are pushed to, just so long as we are pushed to one extreme or the other. At either end, deception and bondage await). At times, with movements that have fallen into error, there can be a rather strange mixture of certain aspects of 'legalism' alongside 'hyper-liberty' teaching. It is amazing what the devil can use to deceive us Christians at times.

When I speak of hyper-grace or hyper-liberty teaching, what I am speaking of is basically an emphasis that is at the exact opposite extreme to legalism. In fact, very often it is essentially a "reaction" against Pharisee-style legalism and all that goes with it. I believe that the hyper-grace emphasis that has had such a great effect on the church over the last ten years or so is largely a reaction against all the heavy domination, legalism and abuse of power that held sway (particularly in Pentecostal circles) throughout much of the seventies and early eighties. While it could be said that legalism essentially involves "judgment without mercy", it could equally be said that 'hyper-grace' largely brings in the opposite extreme: "mercy without judgment". In other words, this emphasis (or should I say, 'unbalanced over-emphasis') revolves far too much around all the 'positive' things like liberty, grace, joy, blessings, total freedom, etc.

The result of this hyper-grace teaching is the exact opposite of what legalism brings: Instead of 'heaviness' and condemnation, we get an increasing amount of spiritual 'license' or casting off of restraint amongst Christians. What is happening here is that, while legalism errs in its excessive emphasis on the "letter" (using Scriptures as 'laws', etc), hyper-grace or hyper-liberty often errs in its excessive emphasis on the "Spirit" (blessings, freedom, experiences, healings, 'touches', etc). In other words, solid Scriptural teaching on repentance, `taking up the cross', holiness and other basic, 'meaty' subjects is toned down or totally de-emphasized, and in its place, spiritual experiences, total liberty in Christ, 'inner healing', etc, are brought to the fore.

In many ways this whole scenario could be likened very much to what took place in the youth culture of the late 1960's. The young people of that time obviously felt "shackled" by the constraints and conservatism of their parents' generation and decided to break free of these shackles entirely, giving full vent to their youthful urges, etc. At first, this must have seemed like a refreshing change, but it wasn't long before these new doctrines of 'true freedom and liberty' amongst the youth began to get dangerously out of hand. All the old authority figures, the old standards, the old values, began to be simply rejected and tossed away – all in the name of "true liberty". The new value system was really very simple: 'If it feels good do it, give in to your impulses, cast off restraint, be free'! This was clearly no longer just innocent youthful exuberance. It had now entered into the realm of out-and-out 'lawlessness' or rebellion. And many of the most damaging and poisonous errors of modern society (which have led to untold misery and deception for millions of people) can now be traced directly back to this so-called 'liberty revolution' of the sixties (mass drug use, 'free love', legalized abortion, hyper-feminism, the New Age, etc).

Some may feel that I am stretching things too far by comparing the current hyper-grace or hyper-liberty emphasis in the church, with the 'liberty revolution' of the late sixties. However, there are in fact many similarities between the two. Both seemingly began as a "reaction" against former constraint and conservatism. Both have involved new teaching on 'true freedom and liberty', and a casting off of the old constraints. Both have brought in an era where the old 'authorities' (i.e., the Scriptures, and good, old-fashioned 'common-sense') no longer necessarily have the real say over what is "acceptable" or not. And both have brought in an era where 'experiences' are often valued more highly than anything the 'old authorities' had to say. Because of this last aspect, in the late sixties the devil was able to bring a tide of demonic Eastern religious beliefs and experiences flooding into the West on an unprecedented scale. It was a massive victory for the devil, and we are still living with the results of this demonic tide in the West today. This would never have been possible without the 'hyper-liberty' emphasis of the youth culture of that time.

I just want to make one thing very clear at this point: I am not against genuine teaching on the true liberty that we have in Christ. What I am against is the extreme over-emphasis of this genuine 'Christian liberty' doctrine. If only today's grace teaching was truly balanced with an emphasis on deep repentance, 'taking up the cross', genuine holiness, Scriptural authority, etc, then I am sure that things would not have reached such a dangerous extreme. There can be no doubt about the deadliness of such religious extremes. There are demonic forces at work here. While it could be said that the 'legalistic' extreme brings Christians under bondage to 'Pharisaical' spirits, it could also be stated that 'hyper-liberty' is almost certain to bring Christians under bondage to 'Jezebel'-type spirits. All the hallmarks are there. Wherever there is the "casting off of authority and restraint" to any real degree, 'Jezebel' will always get involved (especially when it is amongst God's people). She loves to move in on the vacuum created by the diluting or compromising of true spiritual authority (in this case, of the Scriptures as well as the leadership).

In the story of the reign of Israel's king Ahab, it is clear that the queen-witch Jezebel took great advantage of the vacuum created by the king's spiritual compromise and insipid leadership to begin to manipulate and control him (and the entire nation through him). "Doctrines of demons" gradually took over, in the form of open Baal-worship. It is interesting to note that Elijah was the one who was raised up and anointed by God to oppose and destroy the power of Jezebel in the nation. The same thing is about to occur in our day when the new 'Elijah' ministries are raised up and anointed by God. There can be no denying that compromise, the diluting of true spiritual authority, soulishness and the 'casting off of restraint' create a literal "Jezebel's playground" in the church. As I said before, all her hallmarks are now present in many of our churches.

It is interesting to note what occurred when the great leader Moses was called away by God to the top of Mount Sinai for a period. The devil eagerly exploited the vacuum of spiritual authority created by Moses' absence, and the weak, compromising leaders who remained (Aaron and the others) were easily deluded into leading the people into great spiritual error (idolatry, etc). "...and the people sat down to eat and drink, AND ROSE UP TO PLAY" (Ex 32:6). This is certainly a very relevant example of 'casting off restraint'. It is also interesting to note the comments of the great Revival leader John Wesley on one occasion: "ALMOST AS SOON AS I WAS GONE two or three began to take their imaginations for impressions from God. Meantime, a flood of reproach came upon me almost from every quarter..."

As we see from these examples, when true spiritual authority is "absent" from the scene, God's people become easy prey for the devil's deception. It is my belief that many of today's Christian leaders who have imbibed the hyper-grace emphasis, have essentially reacted against the old 'straight-laced' style of Christian leadership, and have instead gone right over to the other extreme (i.e., they have become populist or over-accommodating, wanting to be seen as modern, 'hip', and dynamic. Thus "authority" has become a dirty word).

This, along with the subtle down-grading of the Scriptures as a kind of 'final authority', has resulted in a huge "absence" of real authority in the church, which the devil has been quick to exploit. Fruits of this modern "cool" Christianity are: Worldliness, rebellion, compromise, pride, etc.

The Scripture, "they sat down to eat and drink, and rose up to play" has, in recent years, become very applicable to large sections of the modern church. Many of our young people in particular have never known anything else but a kind of shallow, "good times" Christianity. They can often be found 'raging it up large' at modern youth events and concerts, not because they are just so 'passionate' in their deep worship of God, but rather because they really enjoy riding the shallow "buzz" of the music, etc. Let me be very clear here: This whole "cool" thing comes from the 'spirit of this world', not from God.

And it is not just the youth who have succumbed to this shallow "partying" spirit. Many of the older ones have now also given themselves over to it. Anyone who objects to this "party-time" emphasis in the church is soon labeled sneeringly as being 'legalistic' or judgmental. Like the youth of the sixties, we are now being told to just 'let go', to "yield" to the impulses we receive, etc. We are told that in doing so, we are breaking free from tradition and religion. In actual fact, what we are doing is giving ourselves over, lock, stock and barrel to 'Jezebel', to do with as she pleases. (Remember that I write this as a fairly 'liberated' modern musician myself. I am not at all "anti" most Rock music or youth culture, but I am certainly against the kind of shallow 'casting off of restraint' that we are seeing in today's churches. This can only ever lead to deep deception).

It was Pentecostal pioneer Frank Bartleman who lamented, concerning the early Pentecostal movement: "As the movement began to apostatize platforms were built higher, coat tails were worn longer, choirs were organized, and string bands came into existence to 'jazz' the people. The kings came back once more, to their thrones, restored to sovereignty. We were no longer 'brethren'. Then the divisions multiplied..." And as Samuel Chadwick so insightfully stated: "A religion of mere emotion and sensationalism is the most terrible of all curses that can come upon any people." It had actually been prophesied in the 1906 'Azusa Street' Revival that: "In the last days three things will happen in the great Pentecostal Movement: 1) There will be an overemphasis on power, rather than on righteousness; 2) there will be an overemphasis on praise, to a God they no longer pray to; 3) there will be an overemphasis on the gifts of the Spirit – rather than on the Lordship of Christ."

Today, of course, much of this error is flooding into the church under the guise of "relevance". In the name of 'relevance', we are rushing around desperately trying to make our music "cool" and our leadership style "cool" and our gospel "cool" and our youth events "cool", etc, etc – all in an effort to attract the world on its own terms. Let me say again: None of this is of God at all. It relies almost entirely on the 'arm of the flesh'. It is really nothing less than worldliness, compromise and rebellion in a new and very subtle (yet deadly) form.

Instead of "holier than thou", it seems like we are now expected to be "cooler than thou". Our whole effort is aimed at proving to the world that Christianity is just as cool, just as much shallow fun, just as much of a party, as the world has to offer. And so, to prove all this, we have to entertain and entertain and entertain. We feel we have to become just like the world, in order to impress the world on its own terms. Thus, we now need to be seen in fashionable (or better-still, 'hip' or alternative) clothes. And our youth events become an excuse for a "party". And our presentations become entertaining multi-media extravaganzas. All in an effort to equal or "out-cool" the world (which is why you now see 'stage-diving', etc, at our youth concerts – matching the world on its own mindless, hedonistic terms. "Lovers of pleasures more than lovers of God"). Like I said, cool pride, worldliness and rebellion – all in the name of "relevance". JUST LIKE THE WORLD IN EVERY SENSE. Does this sound like God to you?

As Jesus Himself said: "If you were of the world, the world would love its own; but because you are not of the world, but I chose you out of the world, therefore the world hates you" (Jn 15:19). And as the apostle John wrote: "Love not the world, neither the things that are in the world. If any man love the world, the love of the Father is not in him" (1 Jn 2:15). The apostle James likewise wrote: "Do you not know that friendship with the world is enmity with God? Therefore, whoever wishes to be a friend of the world makes himself an enemy of God" (James 4:4).

This whole "cool Christianity" thing is the complete opposite of the true gospel. The true gospel message involves "denying self, taking up the cross, and following Jesus." But this new gospel of 'cool' says, in essence, "indulge yourself, enjoy it all, look cool, be cool (carnal human pride in all its 'look at me' glory), and have God as well!" The true cross of Jesus speaks death to self, death to hype, death to pride and worldly 'cool', death to loving pleasures more than God. This is why the true gospel and the true message of the cross have always been "foolishness" to carnal man. They speak the OPPOSITE of worldliness – in fact, DEATH to the world! Surely today's Christians can see the difference? ('Cool' is just another name for "pride", after all). I am convinced that what today's youth need is a CHALLENGE worth giving their lives for, not merely another round of mindless 'entertainment'.

The fact is I am a great believer in "relevance" myself. But it must be a relevance that PREACHES THE ORIGINAL GOSPEL WITH ITS ORIGINAL UNCOMPROMISING MESSAGE, using modern means. In other words, the gospel must remain as cross-centered, as convicting and as radical in its demands as it was in the beginning, but the means of transmitting it may change (though never merely for the sake of being 'cool'). I actually believe that

God is going to greatly use the secular media (including the TV networks) to spread news of what He is doing right around the world in the coming Revival. And neither do I mind a certain amount of being "all things to all men" in order to reach the lost (after all, Jesus Himself came as a poor man preaching to poor men). But if our motive for this is to enjoy appearing cool or 'hip'/ alternative, or to appeal to the "God is fun" brigade, then we have gone way too far, and our bowing to the 'spirit of this world' will greatly distort the message that we bring.

I hope you can see that I am by no means advocating some kind of strict, cloistered, "joy-less" Christianity, or a return to the dark days of conformist conservatism in the church. What I am, in fact, advocating is a vibrant, relevant brand of the ORIGINAL NEW TESTAMENT FAITH – updated for the 21st Century, but full of the essence of everything that made the early church what it was. This is clearly the only way that we are ever going to impact this present generation with the life-giving power of the cross of Jesus Christ.

I believe that the Christianity that is coming will be truly 'liberated' and yet completely unpretentious and down-to-earth (rather than 'hip'-cool or 'party'-fun). It will be a gritty, street-level faith – truly 'in the world but not of it' – reaching out to the "man on the street", and utterly glorifying to God.

Probably more than at any time in history, we have a crying need today for searching, convicting 'repentance' preaching in the churches. The Laodicean church is in desperate need of some good, old-fashioned 'Revival' preaching on "sin, righteousness and judgment" (Jn 16:8). This is why I believe that Revival and Reformation are now so urgent. I do not believe that God can live with a compromised Laodicean church. There can be little doubt that He is about to take drastic action (as He has done many times in the past). Today's church should be on her knees, begging God for forgiveness, not "partying up large". But again we hear her cry: "I am rich and increased with goods, and have need of nothing."

Sick, selfish, lukewarm church – do you not care that God has promised to "spew" you out of His mouth?

In the next chapter we will be looking at past Reformations and Revivals, and the very applicable lessons that we can learn from them with today's situation in mind. But firstly I want to briefly discuss some keys that I believe God has given me regarding how to deal effectively with any religious 'strongholds' in our lives. In this chapter we have looked in some detail at the religious strongholds that can exist in the lives of Christians – both at the 'legalistic' extreme and also at the 'hyper-liberty' end of the scale. In dealing with such strongholds in my own life, God has given me a number of principles that are very effective in up-rooting or destroying not only 'religious' strongholds, but other kinds also.

If, having read about the various aspects of 'religion' in this chapter, you believe that it is possible you are being affected by one or more religious strongholds deep within you, then the first thing to do is to pray and ask God to shed light on every aspect of this stronghold. You must be willing to be totally transparent before God in this, and brutally honest with yourself. As with any kind of godly refining or repentance, it can often 'hurt' to suddenly be faced with some of the darkness that exists in one's own heart or soul. But this is an essential part of the process. We must ask God to shed light on any area of darkness within us that needs to be dealt with (whether it is spiritual pride, judgmentalism, striving, or whatever).

The next step in dealing with each stronghold (and it is important that they be dealt with one by one) may well be to ask God's forgiveness, particularly if this stronghold has caused you to hurt or offend others. The third step (and this is very important) is to "RENOUNCE" this stronghold by name, not just with your mouth, but FROM THE DEPTHS OF YOUR HEART AND YOUR WHOLE BEING, IN THE NAME OF JESUS CHRIST. What you are doing here is utterly 'rejecting' this stronghold, casting it away from you as a 'hated' thing, not just with your heart and mind, but from the depths of your soul and your whole being, in Jesus' name.

Because you want God to 'reign' in every part of you, you are violently up-rooting and casting away this stronghold of darkness within you. This area will now become a new stronghold of Godliness in your life – where "God's will is done", where His 'kingdom' is established in a part of you that was previously allied with darkness, and which the enemy was once able to use to manipulate you. And the fruit of the Spirit (love, joy, peace, etc), will now reign in this area far more than they ever have before.

This same process of "RENOUNCING AND VIOLENTLY CASTING DOWN STRONGHOLDS IN JESUS' NAME" can also be used in dealing with other areas of darkness in one's life: self-pity (the cause of much depression), rage, lust, rebellion, false doctrines, 'wounds' or resentments from the past, etc. In dealing with these things it is necessary to be TOTALLY RUTHLESS in rooting them out. We must not make 'pets' out of any of them. (For instance, some people secretly "enjoy" self-pity, and will cultivate it for hours. If they are ever to be truly free of it, then they must be quite RUTHLESS with this stronghold. The same goes for all of these things. We must be prepared to be brutally honest with ourselves).

About three years ago, when God showed me these principles, He led me through a period of about three days where I was asking Him to reveal and shed light on any of these kinds of strongholds in my life. Over these three days, many of these strongholds were 'RENOUNCED' and totally up-rooted and destroyed from out of my life. (Many of them were areas of darkness that I had been struggling to get complete victory over for years). It was so simple! My whole Christian walk was totally transformed within just three days. I was literally a new person. Glory to God! And I have never since reverted back to my old state. (By the way, I still remain on the lookout for any of these strongholds trying to reestablish themselves again. It's like a garden – "weeding" will be required at times, and there is always more 'land' to be taken!)

Really, the major principle that we are speaking of here, is the use of the "sword of the Spirit" (the word of God), which is the possession of every Spirit-filled believer, to violently lay siege to spiritual strongholds of darkness deep within us. (On a personal level, I believe that many of these strongholds have their roots in the fallen 'soul' area of man. This is why we must "RENOUNCE" them from the depths of our hearts and souls). The Bible speaks of the word of God as being a sharp two-edged sword, a consuming fire, and a hammer that breaks the rock into pieces. What we are doing here is using this God-given authority to cast down spiritual strongholds in Jesus' name. And wherever an enemy stronghold is cast down, the 'kingdom of God' is established.

Essentially, this could be understood in terms of a kind of spiritual equivalent, on an infinitesimal scale, of Joshua taking the land of Canaan "by force" – casting down the enemy strongholds (Jericho, Ai, etc), and marching in to 'possess the land' in the name of the Lord (i.e., establishing the 'kingdom of God' in the land, in His name). This is the exact principle that will be behind much of the coming Revival also. As Jesus declared, "From the days of John the Baptist until now, the kingdom of heaven suffers violence, and the violent take it by force" (Mt 11:12).

I believe that the above principle applies in exactly the same way on a global level as it does on a personal level: God giving His servants a special authority and anointing to take territory away from the enemy and to establish His 'kingdom' there instead. What we are now awaiting, is for the new, anointed "Joshuas" to arise in the earth, with the authority and power from God to cast down these global enemy strongholds (and the lies that go with them) – to spiritually 'take the kingdom by force'. Glory to God! This is exactly what the coming Revival will be all about.

Chapter Four

REVIVAL!

Through the years, as I have studied accounts of many past Revivals, it has become more and more apparent to me that many of today's ideas about what Revival actually is are not only inadequate, but also often damaging and misleading. Many Christians see Revival only as a time of great celebration, joy and 'harvest'. They do not realize that these things are the "fruit" that FOLLOW AFTER true Revival. True Revival itself is aimed at cleansing, purging and then empowering God's people. If His people have fallen into a state of spiritual decline or bankruptcy, then the first thing that true Revival will bring is a tremendous conviction of sin and deep repentance. The whole idea is to see these Christians convicted and cleansed, so that they can once again become clean channels to bring God's blessing and salvation to a dying world – so that they can once again fully display His glory in all the earth. True Revival brings God's children to their knees. As one writer commented, Revival is "not the top blowing off, but rather the bottom falling out." And as Frank Bartleman wrote, 'The depth of revival will be determined exactly by the depth of the spirit of repentance.'

It is not uncommon, in times of Revival, for people to be so stricken with conviction of sin by the Holy Spirit that they are literally unable to do anything except lie face-down and cry out to God for mercy, in the greatest distress, until assured by Him that they have received His forgiveness. (Usually, especially in the early stages of Revival, these will be CHRISTIANS who have been harboring sin of some kind in their lives). Sometimes they may even feel the need to confess their sin publicly before forgiveness and cleansing can take place. We must never forget that Revival is firstly aimed at the CHRISTIANS. As history clearly shows, it is a flood of deep cleansing, REPENTANCE and empowering aimed at "reviving" God's people, so that they can bring in a mighty 'harvest'.

The following is a description of some of the Revival prayer-meetings that took place in the Welsh Revival of 1858-59 (typical of many Revivals): "It was in its terrors that the eternal became a reality to them first. They seemed plunged into depths of godly sorrow... For some weeks it was the voice of weeping and the sound of mourning that was heard in the meetings. The house was often so full of the divine presence that ungodly men trembled terror-stricken; and at the close, sometimes they fled as from some impending peril; at other times sat glued to their seats..."

One eyewitness said of the famous 1904 Welsh Revival that it was not the eloquence of Evan Roberts that broke men down, but his tears. "He would break down, crying bitterly for God to bend them, in an agony of prayer, the tears coursing down his cheeks, with his whole frame writhing. Strong men would break down and cry like children... a sound of weeping and wailing would fill the air."

Here is a typical extract from the autobiography of renowned Revivalist Charles G. Finney, concerning a meeting that he held in one particularly ungodly place: "I had not spoken to them in this strain of direct application more than a quarter of an hour when all at once an awful solemnity seemed to settle down upon them. The congregation began to fall from their seats in every direction and cry for mercy. If I had had a sword in each hand I could not have cut them off their seats as fast as they fell. Indeed, nearly the whole congregation were either on their knees or prostrate in less than two minutes from this first shock that fell upon them. Everyone who was able to speak at all prayed for himself... Of course I was obliged to stop preaching, for they no longer paid any attention. I saw the old man who had invited me there to preach, sitting about in the middle of the house and looking around with utter amazement. I raised my voice almost to a scream to make him hear above the noise of the sobbing, and pointing to him said, 'Can't you pray?'..."

In this kind of genuine outpouring of the Holy Spirit, the tangible presence of God is very real. Frank Bartleman described one of the meetings during the 'Azusa Street' Revival of 1906 as follows: "God came so wonderfully near us the very atmosphere of Heaven seemed to surround us. Such a divine "weight of glory" was upon us we could only lie on our faces. For a long time we could hardly remain seated even. All would be on their faces on the floor, sometimes during the whole service. I was seldom able to keep from lying full length on the floor on my face."

This overwhelming sense of being in the awesome presence, the "shekinah glory" of a holy God, brings agonizing conviction of sin to those whose hearts are not right with Him, but also great rejoicing and true joy to the ones who know they have been washed clean. These extremes of great sorrow over sin, followed by genuine 'joy unspeakable', often bring accusations of "emotionalism" and hysteria from those who oppose the Revival. However, it has been found that deep and genuine moves of God that begin with deep conviction of sin, and result in deep joy, have always produced sound and lasting fruit wherever they have occurred.

Many Revivals have resulted in such overwhelming joy, praise and jubilation in those newly forgiven, that bystanders have often been astonished at the shouts of glory to God, the unrestrained worship and singing, etc. It is important to remember however, that such "righteousness, peace and joy in the Holy Spirit" is only truly possible amongst those who have come to this place by way of brokenness and deep repentance. There must always be 'death' before there can be 'resurrection'.

As Evan Roberts (of the 1904 Welsh Revival) said: "First, is there any sin in your past with which you have not honestly dealt, not confessed to God? On your knees at once. Your past must be put away and cleansed. Second, is there anything in your life that is doubtful – anything you cannot decide whether it is good or evil? Away with it. There must not be a trace of a cloud between you and God. Have you forgiven everybody – EVERYBODY? If not, don't expect forgiveness for your sins..." There can be no denying that deep repentance and prayer are truly the keys to genuine Revival. This has been the case with every previous outpouring, and it will undoubtedly be the same with this coming one also.

A CLOUD OF CONFUSION...

With any new move of God, Satan is desperate to somehow thwart or destroy it, not just AFTER it has begun, but if at all possible, even BEFORE it begins. We see this, for instance, in the lives of both Moses and Jesus. In both of these cases, the devil attempted to kill these "chosen ones" (who were to become leaders of two of the greatest moves of God of all time), by having all the infants that were their age put to death. In both cases, Satan saw all the signs of a coming great move of God, and he wanted to "nip it in the bud", so to speak, before it could really begin. The devil will use any means at his disposal to try and derail or destroy a new (or imminent) Revival. As history shows, one of his favorite tricks is to try to bury the new move under a great barrage of counterfeits, confusion and lies.

The devil has seen enough of Revival in the past to loathe and fear it in the extreme. Revival is the devil's worst nightmare come true – a flood of cleansing and power designed to restore God's people to being what they are meant to be in the world: a potent threat to Satan's kingdom and all his works. When Revival breaks out, or is about to break out, the devil will often move on many fronts: targeting certain leaders whom God is using to prepare the people (for if a major leader falls, then the devil is able to bring in great deception), trying to break up relationships between key leaders, stirring up opposition from other Christians, introducing "counterfeits" on as large a scale as possible, stirring up controversy to distract people's minds away from central truths, etc. If he can ruin a Revival in the 'preparation' stage, then the devil knows he has done incredibly well. However, if he can't, then he will try to ruin it as soon as possible after it begins. Dirty tactics are the order of the day here. The bigger the cloud of confusion, rumors and counterfeits, the happier the devil will be. In short, he will do anything at all to try and discredit or hinder a new (or imminent) move of God (especially if it is the great end-times Revival!)

It was John Wesley who said, "Be not alarmed that Satan sows tares among the wheat of Christ. It has ever been so, especially on any remarkable outpouring of the Spirit; and ever will be, until the devil is chained for a thousand years. Till then he will always ape, and endeavor to counteract the work of the Spirit of Christ." Counterfeits are very common in times of Revival: counterfeit manifestations, counterfeit conversions, counterfeit so-called "Revival" preachers, preaching the most extreme or distorted doctrines, etc. All used unwittingly by the devil to discredit or hinder the real Revival. As Adam Clarke said: "...in great revivals of religion, it is almost impossible to prevent wild-fire from getting in among the true fire."

One of the devil's favorite tricks in times of Revival is to push some of the 'pro-Revival' ministries to real extremes in their preaching and ministering, etc, so as to discredit the whole move of God because of them. As Frank Bartleman wrote, "Man always adds to the message God has given. This is Satan's chief way to discredit and destroy it. Both Luther and Wesley had the same difficulties to contend with. And so has every God given revival... The message generally suffers more from its friends than from its foes." John Wesley once prayed, "Oh, Lord, send us the old revival, without the defects; but if this cannot be, send it – with all its defects. We must have the revival."

As I said, counterfeit spiritual manifestations are very common in times of Revival. These are often caused by believers seeking after 'touches', blessings or experiences, etc, rather than seeking God for His own sake. It is very dangerous for Christians to seek after anything but a deeper and purer relationship with God Himself. Any seeking after mere 'touches' or experiences is really nothing but "soulishness", and can result in great spiritual deception. As always, a certain number of such false manifestations or counterfeit experiences will be merely fleshly, while others will be downright demonic. In fact, this is real "JEZEBEL" territory (especially if the manifestations involve a 'casting off of restraint' or a kind of "wildness"). Sometimes, in extreme cases, it is possible for whole movements to become 'given over' to these kinds of counterfeit manifestations, etc.

However, it is also important to remember that God Himself often does 'unusual' things in times of Revival. For instance, sudden, massive outpourings of the Holy Spirit will often result in tremendous outcryings of distress over sin or 'trembling' under the fear of God, then (when repentance and forgiveness have taken place) outbursts of joyous praise and thanksgiving, etc. They may also result in mass 'speaking in tongues', falling down under the power of God, dreams, visions, angelic visitations, etc.

A large number of these things can be easily counterfeited by the devil, of course, so it is vital that the leaders are well able to discern what is false and what is true. One of the devil's favorite tricks in times of real Revival is to mix as many counterfeit manifestations as possible into what God is doing, thus causing many observers to discredit the whole thing as being 'not of God'.

However, if such counterfeits are not causing large-scale problems, then it can be best for the leaders not to draw too much attention to them. (Attempting to loudly 'correct' relatively small-scale problems can sometimes make the people overly suspicious of ANYTHING unusual, thus making it hard for the Holy Spirit to work as well). However, if these counterfeits are flooding in on a large scale, then it will be necessary for the leaders to bring open correction, using all the authority that God has given them. If such authority and correction is 'absent' from this kind of situation, then the devil will quickly get in and take complete control. This is why 'soft' or compromising leaders are so deadly in times of Revival. How easily Satan can manipulate them for his purposes!

I believe that the leadership in the coming Revival will be very wary of encouraging soulishness in any way. I certainly can't imagine them using the kind of "tugging at the heart-strings" techniques so often seen today. All that is showy, all that is soulish, all that is shallow and that would wrap people up in a warm, positive, "feel-good" cocoon – all this God hates. And yet this kind of thing seems to have been so common in recent years. In my experience, very few Christians even seem to be able to tell this kind of Christianity from the real thing anymore.

The new Revival ministries will detest this kind of soulishness, hype and emotional manipulation. Their preaching (and their singing) will certainly not be in demonstration of personality, cleverness or showmanship, but rather, "in demonstration of the Spirit and of power" (1 Cor 2:4). And I believe that the 'new music' that will accompany this Revival will also be completely free of any thought of manipulating people's emotions in any way. However, despite all this, I have no doubt that the coming Revival will be accused of 'emotionalism' and hysteria, just like all those that have gone before.

REFORMATION – A 'NEW WINESKIN'

Whenever God feels that it is vital that a new Revival is completely removed from the influence of the old leaders and the old church systems, etc, then He will bring about not just a Revival, but a total "REFORMATION" – a complete 'leaving behind' of the old structures and leadership, etc. This is clearly what God has stated will occur in the coming move of God. Really, the principle behind this concept of "total reformation" is the same as that described by Jesus Himself in Lk 5:37-38: "... no man puts new wine into old wineskins, else the new wine will burst the wineskins and be spilled, and the wineskins will perish. But new wine must be put into new wineskins."

Church history often underlines the great folly of trying to preserve the 'new wine' in the old skins. How many Revivals down the centuries have literally 'bled to death', simply because men have tried to cram the 'new wine' into the old church systems and structures, etc? Often, all this has meant is that the Revival has been relatively short-lived, and has often failed to fully accomplish all that God had purposed for it. Really, the most effective and long-lived Revivals have been the ones that not only involved great outpourings of the Holy Spirit, but also the 'leaving behind' of the old church systems (and all that went with them), and the formation of a 'new movement' with new leaders, etc. Some well-known examples of this are the 'Great Reformation' under Martin Luther, the Wesley Revivals of the eighteenth century, and last century's "Salvation Army" Revivals under William Booth (not to mention the original "Book-of-Acts" Revival itself).

All of these Revivals were really also 'Reformations', involving the leaving behind of the "old" systems, and the establishing of entirely 'new' movements, with new leaders.

The desire to stay with the "old", to stick to what you know and feel comfortable with, to try and cram the new move of God into the existing structures, etc, is often a great temptation. However, this kind of 'comfort zone' mentality really has to go. It can be a deadly threat to the effectiveness and longevity of any Revival. If we are going to see a genuine move of God's Spirit in these last days that will truly sweep the world, then we had better get used to the idea, not only of the 'new wine', but also of the 'new wineskin' that will go with it.

We have already spoken at some length of the coming "street-church", or 'street-based' Revival movement. In many ways I believe that this will be very similar to the Book of Acts – a simple, effective, largely house-based and street-based move of God. It will involve huge open-air meetings where the new apostles and prophets will speak (with 'signs and miracles' following) and where the 'new music' will be heard. And it will also involve small local gatherings of believers (usually from 'house to house'), where local Christians will come together to pray, partake of the Lord's Supper, exercise spiritual gifts, etc: "When you come together, each one of you has a song, a teaching, a revelation, a tongue or an interpretation. Let all things be done for edification" (1 Cor 14:26). The leaders of these house gatherings will not be there to control or dominate, but rather to make sure that the Holy Spirit is free to move, and that any excesses do not get out of hand. This will be an ideal environment for new believers to begin to exercise their giftings – to 'learn by doing'.

However, as well as discussing the new 'structure' of the coming Revival movement, it is important to remember that God's true Church is an 'organism', not an organization. The true Church is built out of PEOPLE – God's "living stones". It is not built out of new 'meeting' formats or differently-designed 'boxes'. The important thing is the PEOPLE. THEY are what make up God's Church. We are told in Eph 2:20 that the true Church is "built on the foundation of the apostles and prophets", with Jesus Himself as the "cornerstone, in whom the whole structure is joined together and grows into a holy temple in the Lord." In other words, the Church is built out of PEOPLE, with Jesus as the 'cornerstone' and His apostles and prophets as the 'foundation' upon which it is built. Every Reformation and Revival in history has been built on the new 'apostles and prophets' that God has raised up for that hour. And this one will be no different. God has made it very clear that it is "WHEN THE NEW APOSTLES ARISE" that the coming Reformation and Revival will truly begin.

Just like the early Church, this is to be an 'apostolic' move. (i.e., it will revolve around the teaching and ministry of the new apostles that are about to arise). "And they devoted themselves to the apostles' teaching and fellowship, to the breaking of bread and to prayer. And fear came upon every soul; and many wonders and signs were done through the apostles... And the Lord added to their number daily those who were being saved." (Acts 2:42-47). In fact, every one of the 'five-fold' ministries will be abundantly represented in this Revival: Apostles, prophets, evangelists, shepherds and teachers, "to equip the saints for the work of ministry, for building up the body of Christ... to mature manhood, to the measure of the stature of the fullness of Christ" (Eph 4:11-13). These ministries are like the foundations and 'supporting beams' of God's Church, around which the whole body is built, so that it can grow up into the 'full stature' of Christ.

One thing is for sure: Jesus Christ will truly be 'Head' of His Church in this Revival. Though the new apostles will be appointed to lead His Church in His name, it will be JESUS who will be in charge, and it is HE whom the new ministries will be constantly looking to for direction, etc. This is to be the Church's finest hour. She will be the most radiant, the most glorious Bride in all history – pure and holy, without 'spot or wrinkle or any such thing'. God has saved the 'best wine' – the greatest anointing – for last for this move. We live in the days of the greatest Revival in the history of the world, and the last great "harvest", immediately preceding the greatest JUDGEMENT that the earth has ever seen. And we live in the era of the most anointed 'street-church' in Revival history. As God has said, "I am going to change the understanding and expression of Christianity IN THE EARTH in one generation." Tell me Christians, are you ready for this? "And they overcame him {the devil} by the blood of the Lamb, and by the word of their testimony; AND THEY LOVED NOT THEIR LIVES UNTO THE DEATH" (Rev 12:11).

REVIVAL LEADERS

In studying many past moves of God, it soon became apparent to me that there were often striking similarities between the various men that God had chosen to lead His people in times of Reformation and Revival. In fact, the spiritual lineage of such men stretches way back to the "mighty men" of old – Joshua, Caleb, Moses, Gideon, Elijah, John the Baptist, etc – men of great daring and renown – all the way down through the apostles and on to Savonarola, Luther, Whitfield, Wesley, Edwards, Finney, William Booth, Evan Roberts, Jonathan Goforth, John Sung, Smith Wigglesworth, etc, etc. All were men who had "paid the price", who had spent much time alone in secret with God, and often years in the 'wilderness' before being anointed with power from on high and sent forth to loose God's people from their chains of bondage and sin. Suddenly they arrived, as if from nowhere, utterly fearless and with a searing message that pierced straight to the hearts of their hearers. This is the way it has always been and ever will be, with such "anointed ones" of God.

As A.W. Tozer has said, "God has always had His specialists... who appeared at critical moments in history to reprove, rebuke and exhort in the name of God and righteousness... Such a man was likely to be drastic, radical, possibly at times violent, and the curious crowd that gathered to watch him work soon branded him as extreme, fanatical, negative. And in a sense they were right. He was single-minded, severe, fearless, and these were the qualities the circumstances demanded. He shocked some, frightened others and alienated not a few, but he knew who had called him and what he was sent to do. His ministry was geared to the emergency, and that fact marked him out as different, a man apart."

The training ground for such men is often deep in the "wilderness" of brokenness, 'nothingness' and death to self. As the historian D'Aubigne wrote, "A great work of God is never accomplished by the natural strength of man. It is from the dry bones, the darkness and the dust of death, that God is pleased to select the instruments by means of which He designs to scatter over the earth His light, regeneration and life."

Yet another writer has observed, "In the various crises that have occurred in the history of the church, men have come to the front who have manifested a holy recklessness that astonished their fellows. When Luther nailed his theses to the door of the cathedral at Wittemburg, cautious men were astonished at his audacity. When John Wesley ignored all church restrictions and religious propriety and preached in the fields and by-ways, men declared his reputation was ruined. So it has been in all ages... An utter recklessness concerning men's opinions and other consequences is the only attitude that can meet the exigencies of the present times."

Such men as these were often the most controversial figures of their day. They were loved by some and utterly loathed by others.

They were usually perceived as a threat to the status quo, the church "establishment", and so were often treated with great suspicion – even hatred – by those in power. These were men who had battled through in prayer, right into the very throne-room of God. There they had tasted of the heavenly glory, and had been imbued with a vision and a passion far beyond mere words. And now they were dangerous men – men on fire with love and devotion toward a holy God. Never again would they be satisfied with a church that did not fully display His glory and His majesty to a dying world. Never again would they allow their Saviour to be left, "wounded in the house of His friends."

These Reformers and Revivalists were men who had surrendered all to God, who had been willing to pay any price to see God arise and scatter His enemies in the earth. They had willingly allowed themselves to be humbled and broken by Him, so that they might one day become true instruments of His glory. They were truly dead to 'self', dead to sin, "dead to the world and all its toys, its idle pomp and fading joys". They were alive only to Jesus, and His word burned in their hearts as a consuming fire, and in their mouths as a two-edged sword.

REVIVAL PREACHING

It is a well-known fact that the old Revivalists used to often preach searchingly and fearlessly on "sin, righteousness and judgment". There is a very good reason for this: Jesus had specifically stated that the Holy Spirit would CONVICT of these very things – "sin, righteousness and judgment"! (Jn 16:8). The whole purpose of these men's preaching was to unleash the convicting power of the Holy Spirit upon their hearers. They aimed to thoroughly awaken the consciences of the people. Welsh Revivalist Humphrey Jones once urged a young preacher: "...to preach with severity and conviction; aiming continually at the conscience; charging the people with their sins to their very face; having no regard for men's good or bad opinions; and avoiding the exhibition of self during the delivery of your sermon." Now THAT is Revival preaching!

These men would wield God's word under a mighty anointing, not as some kind of blunt weapon to bludgeon people with, but rather as an incisive, precision instrument, a "sharp, two-edged sword", piercing deep into men's hearts, exposing hidden sins, motives and desires, and bringing true godly sorrow and deep repentance. What these preachers were looking for was a "broken heart and a contrite spirit". As with Peter on the day of Pentecost, they preached with a view to seeing men 'cut to the heart', for only then could they be sure that the resulting repentance would be both truly deep and truly lasting.

This has almost always been the character of true Revival preaching, from the days of the apostles right down to the present. On the day of Pentecost it was Peter accusing the Jews to their faces of 'crucifying the Messiah' that caused them to be 'cut to the heart', and to cry out, "Men and brethren, what shall we do?" (Acts 2:36-37). And the record states that three thousand people were converted that day after hearing this one, Spirit-fired sermon. Later in the book of Acts we read of Paul's fearless preaching to governor Felix: "And as he reasoned of righteousness, temperance and judgment to come, FELIX TREMBLED..." (Acts 24:25). And for another Scriptural example of this kind of bold, convicting preaching, we can turn to the martyr Stephen: "'You stiff-necked and uncircumcised in heart and ears, you always resist the Holy Spirit: as your fathers did, so do you'..." (Acts 7:51-53). There are many further examples of this kind of preaching throughout the New Testament (in the ministries of Jesus and John the Baptist, for instance).

Revival preaching is almost never designed to be deliberately offensive. However it is often extremely direct and utterly fearless. And, as one writer has noted, "fearless" preaching of this kind seems calculated to produce either deep conviction or "the bitterest animosity" (often both!). The old Revivalists were men of enormous godly authority, and they used God's word as a sword to 'lay siege' to the strongholds of sin, compromise and religion that were binding His people. This was never 'comfortable' preaching (for "sin, righteousness and judgment" are not comfortable subjects). However, these men well knew that "the fear of the Lord is the beginning of wisdom" (Pr 9:10). And they preached it as such.

As Martin Luther said: "I was born to fight devils and factions. It is my business to remove obstructions, to cut down thorns, to fill up quagmires, and to open and make straight paths. But if I must have some failing let me rather speak the truth with too great severity than once to act the hypocrite and conceal the truth." And the great Revivalist Charles Finney said of one typical meeting: "The Spirit of God came upon me with such power that it was like opening a battery upon them. For more than an hour, and perhaps for an hour and a half, the word of God came through me to them in a manner that I could see was carrying all before it. It was a fire and a hammer breaking the rock, and as a sword that was piercing to the dividing asunder of soul and spirit. I saw that a general conviction was spreading over the whole congregation. Many of them could not hold up their heads."

Renowned eighteenth century Revivalist Jonathan Edwards (preacher of the famous Revival sermon, "Sinners in the hands of an angry God") noted that the two outstanding features of genuine Revival were great conviction followed by great praise and rejoicing. The following are the characteristics that he himself observed: "(a) An extraordinary sense of the awful majesty, greatness and holiness of God so as sometimes to overwhelm soul and body, a sense of the piercing, all-seeing eye of God so as to sometimes take away the bodily strength; and an extraordinary view of the infinite terribleness of the wrath of God, together with the ineffable misery of sinners exposed to this wrath. (b) Especially longing after these two things; to be more perfect in humility and adoration... The person felt a great delight in singing praises to God and Jesus Christ, and longing that this present life may be as it were one continued song of praise to God..."

The Revivalists of old often preached under such an incredible anointing that the house would be literally full of the wailing cries and sobs of those stricken by God's Spirit. One eyewitness wrote of Savonarola's preaching that it caused "such terror and alarm, such sobbing and tears that people passed through the streets without speaking, more dead than alive"! Some modern Christians, totally unused to this kind of preaching, might say that such an emphasis on "sin, righteousness and judgment" is way over the top. However, in circumstances such as those found in today's church, this kind of preaching is EXACTLY what is needed. This is why God has so often seen fit to raise up and employ this kind of preaching in conditions very similar to today.

The old Revivalists were so full of God's presence, so saturated with His glory, so endued with power from on high, that Revival literally followed them wherever they went. They would never have dared to preach the way they did without this anointing (for 'the letter kills but the Spirit gives life'). But how exactly did they obtain such a mighty anointing? Well, as most of the old records show, it was largely through agonizing, prevailing PRAYER that they had broken through into this realm of real 'Revival' power in their ministry.

REVIVAL PRAYING

Charles Finney said, "... unless I had the spirit of prayer I could do nothing. If I lost the spirit of grace and supplication even for a day or an hour I found myself unable to preach with power and efficiency, or to win souls by personal conversation." George Whitefield said: "Whole days and WEEKS have I spent prostrate on the ground in silent or vocal prayer..." Frank Bartleman wrote: "At night I could scarcely sleep for the spirit of prayer... Prayer literally consumed me." And D.M. McIntyre wrote: "Before the great revival in Gallneukirchen broke out, Martin Boos spent hours and days and often nights in lonely agonies of intercession. Afterwards, when he preached, his words were as flame, and the hearts of the people as grass."

This was urgent, anointed, Spirit-fired praying, led and inspired by God. The old Revivalists used to speak of the spirit of prayer being "outpoured" upon them. They spoke of weeping, agonizing, pleading, wrestling, 'travailing' in prayer. The whole reason that these Revival preachers were so saturated with the glory and the presence of God was because they had truly broken through, right into His very throne-room in prayer, and had spent much time communing with Him there. Deep repentance, daring faith, and 'agonizing', Spirit-fired prayer have always been the keys to genuine Revival in any age (and this, of course, applies to everybody, not just to those in ministry).

As history shows, the church can only ever expect true Revival when at least a remnant of God's people truly get DESPERATE – desperate about the backslidden state of the church, desperate about the lukewarmness within them and all around them, desperate about sin and compromise, desperate about the fact that GOD IS NOT GLORIFIED, that He is not truly LORD of His church, that His words are mocked and largely seen as irrelevant by a dying world. Revival will come when God's people truly humble themselves, when they replace their 'positive imaging' ("Rise up, you people of power", etc), with the reality of James' lament: "Be afflicted, and mourn, and weep: let your laughter be turned to mourning, and your joy to heaviness. Humble yourselves in the sight of the Lord, and He shall lift you up" (Ja 4:9-10). We all need to stop playing games and get serious with God. I really believe He is calling us to get 'desperate' about our plight before Him.

In the coming Revival, as with all Revivals, God will no doubt raise up particular intercessors who will 'specialize' in prayer. But really, such praying is for everyone. It was Matthew Henry who said, "When God intends great mercy for His people, the first thing He does is set them a-praying." And Leonard Ravenhill wrote that "the man who can get believers to praying would, under God, usher in the greatest revival that the world has ever known." God will often gather His people together (at least in twos and threes, and often more) to pray down a Revival – just like Pentecost itself. As A.T. Pierson wrote, "From the day of Pentecost, there has been not one great spiritual awakening in any land which has not begun in a union of prayer, though only among two or three; no such outward, upward movement has continued after such prayer meetings declined."

John Wesley said: "Have you any days of fasting and prayer? Storm the throne of grace and persevere therein, and mercy will come down." And Charles Finney declared: "Revival comes from heaven when heroic souls enter the conflict determined to win or die – or if need be, to win and die!" Brothers, sisters, we need to get DESPERATE about Revival!

REVIVAL IN THE COMMUNITY

Once the Christians who heed God's call have been through the fire of His refining, purifying and cleansing, and have received His mighty anointing, then it becomes time for the community at large to experience this great 'invasion' of God's Revival power also. This is when the 'harvest' will truly begin. This is the time for the church to fearlessly invade Satan's kingdom under a mighty anointing, 'releasing the captives' as they go. For those who have experienced God's cleansing and forgiveness, such a time can literally be like "heaven on earth". One writer described Revival as being "a community saturated with God". And Jonathan Edwards said of the 1735 New England Revival, "The town seemed to be full of the presence of God. It was never so full of love, or so full of joy; and yet, so full of distress as it was then."

When Revival spreads out into the community in this way, it is not uncommon for bars to be transformed into prayer meetings, for large numbers of notorious criminals to be converted, and for judges to be left without cases to put to trial! Such is the impact of a mighty general outpouring of the Spirit of God. This is the kind of result that we can expect in the coming great move of God also. Really, these kinds of things are what the church should be seeing on a large scale all the time, but at the moment the 'channels' of such blessing are almost completely blocked by sin and compromise, etc, within the church.

REVIVAL PIONEERS

There can be little doubt that worldwide Revival is now truly "imminent" (after all, this has been prophesied in many nations). But how can individual Christians prepare for such a powerful move of God's Spirit? The answer is really very simple: To be truly ready to play a part in any new move of God, it is necessary to first experience PERSONAL REVIVAL in your own life. In other words, it is necessary to have already been "revived" yourself. This "personal Revival" process involves seeking God with all your heart, ridding your life of any 'cloud' that may be coming between you and God (and asking Him to reveal anything else that He wants dealt with), brokenness, and 'agonizing' prayer (that God would outpour His Spirit upon you and fill you with His faith, His love, His word, His anointing, etc). As Robert Murray McCheyne said, "a holy minister is an awful weapon in the hands of God."

Before any Revival begins, God spends much time (often many years) training His "pioneers", preparing them (often in some secluded spiritual backwater) for the day when His Spirit will be outpoured and they will explode out of the wilderness and onto the world stage with a searing message and a holy boldness that will kindle fire in the hearts of all who hear them. As Frank Bartleman wrote of the Pentecostal pioneers who were gathered for the 'Azusa Street' outpouring, "they were largely called and prepared for years... They had been burnt out, tried and proven... They had walked with God and learned deeply of His Spirit. These were pioneers, 'shock troops', the Gideon's three hundred, to spread the fire around the world. Just as the disciples had been prepared by Jesus." He also observed that, "A body must be prepared, in repentance and humility, for every outpouring of the Spirit."

As Arthur Booth-Clibborn wrote: "The company in the upper room, upon whom Pentecost fell, had paid for it the highest price. In this they approached as near as possible to Him who had paid the supreme price in order to send it. Do we ever really adequately realize how utterly lost to this world, how completely despised, rejected and outcast was that company?... Their Calvary was complete, and so a complete Pentecost came to match it. The latter will resemble the former in completeness. We may, therefore, each of us say to ourselves: As thy cross, so will thy Pentecost be."

It is my belief that God is still looking for Christians to join the ranks of His "Gideon's three hundred" for this Revival: "And I sought for a man among them, that should make up the hedge, and stand in the gap before me for the land..." (Ez 22:30). "For the eyes of the Lord run to and fro throughout the whole earth, to show Himself strong on behalf of them whose heart is perfect toward Him" (2 Ch 16:9). Are YOU willing to become one of those who "stand in the gap" before the Lord? Are you willing to suffer the reproach and the rejection of others as you take your stand with Him? And are you truly willing to 'pay the price', to 'take up your cross' no matter what the cost? The Bible tells us that Jesus was "a man of sorrows, and acquainted with grief." It is only those who are prepared and praying who will be involved in this Revival from the beginning. And for the pioneers, in many ways this will mean "loving not their lives unto the death". A true pioneer's most pressing desire will be to SEE GOD GLORIFIED in every conceivable way. This has always been the purest motive for desiring Revival in any age. And I believe that God is still seeking those who will 'stand in the gap' before Him for this present generation. Tell me, friend, might you be one of these?

Chapter Five

THE SIN OF REBELLION

There may be some readers who think that in discussing the coming Reformation, I have been guilty of inciting 'rebellion against authority'. This is far from the truth. In fact, as this chapter will show, I am very keen to uphold all God-appointed authority. However, due to the seriousness of today's situation and the strong prophetic warnings that God has been giving right around the world, I would have been very remiss not to strongly warn today's leaders of what God has been saying. I only wish that things were different, and that I did not have to say many of the things that I do.

No Revivalist that I have ever read about was a 'popularity'-oriented, or 'man-pleasing' type of leader (in fact, usually quite the opposite!). These were certainly not men to be trifled with. They knew when to be gentle, but were also never afraid to "reprove, rebuke and exhort" with all godly authority where necessary. They were strong yet balanced leaders – firm but fair. Their love for God and for the people (in that order) enabled them to make allowances for people's frailties, but also meant that they never gave the devil an inch. Such mightily anointed leaders as these are sorely needed in our day, and there can be no doubt that this is exactly the kind of leadership that is about to arise in the coming Revival. (For God must have His 'men of valor' – His Joshuas, Elijahs, Gideons, etc, to lead His people on to victory, just as the devil has his 'heroes' also).

However, while we may know and look forward to many of these aspects of the coming move of God, the fact is that most of us are still having to deal with the 'old' set-up, the church system as it exists today. And no doubt many of us have struggled with exactly how we are to approach our relationship with this current set-up. What should our attitudes be towards today's church leaders, for instance, in situations in which we are personally involved? How would God have us relate to these leaders? And how can we recognize the seeds of 'rebellion' in our hearts? These are very important questions, and they are some of the major points that we will be discussing in this chapter.

In working through these issues in my own life, God has very clearly pointed me to the well-known "rebellion" lesson contained in the story of David. What I want to do in this chapter is to take a fresh look at the story of David, Saul and Jonathan, from a slightly new perspective. One of the main focuses, of course, will be the tremendous godly attitudes that this man David had.

You will no doubt recall how that King Saul had fallen into compromise, presumption and rebellion, and that the prophet Samuel had told Saul that the kingdom would be taken from him and given to another. The prophet then went and anointed David to be the future king. However, there was to be a time of waiting and preparation before David could assume the leadership of Israel. It is my belief that this equates directly to the current situation. I believe that there is definitely a "David company" of future 'leaders of Israel' (i.e., the Church) whom God has been preparing in secret for many years right around the world (these will be the apostles and prophets, etc, of the new move of God). Most of those who are part of this "David company" will already know who they are. Many of them will have received their first or even their second anointing (remembering that David was anointed THREE TIMES before he became leader of all Israel), and will probably already be operating in their calling to some degree.

One thing is certain: This will be a company of PROPHETIC PEOPLE – people whom God has been speaking to about the 'things to come'. Such people will often have great difficulty fitting into the present system, for essentially they will have been "designed" for tomorrow's church, rather than today's. They will often feel like misfits, and may be misunderstood, persecuted and maltreated by those who identify themselves strongly with the present order. Often the powers-that-be will see them as some kind of "threat".

Such was the case with David. For years Saul's jealousy and rage caused him to have to flee for his life. Pursued relentlessly by Saul and his men, David was forced to hide out in caves, in the desert, and for a time even amongst the Philistines! How hurt and lonely he must have felt at times! Here he was, the one whom Samuel had anointed to be the future king of Israel, now an outcast, persecuted, maltreated, slandered... And this went on for years.

But now we come to the part of the story that applies directly to the major theme of this chapter. Remember, Saul was still king over Israel, even though he had already been rejected by God. He was still positioned as the leader of God's people. Now here is the crucial question: What was David's attitude toward Saul all this time? The answer is very simple: David regarded Saul as being the "Lord's Anointed" and he was utterly constant in his deep respect and love toward him. He would make no move to try and wrest the leadership away from Saul (as he could have done). He was very aware of God's timing, and he would make no move to circumvent it. His policy was, "touch not the Lord's anointed". Twice he could easily have killed Saul and the kingdom would have been his, but he chose instead to demonstrate his love and his loyalty toward him. His love for Saul was truly from the 'heart'. When news reached David that Saul was dead, he wept and mourned over him. He had still held out hope for Saul, and had treated him as the rightful leader of God's people, right up until the day that Saul died.

It is my belief that by-and-large, there are essentially three types of leaders or ministries operating in today's Christian world: the 'Sauls', the Jonathans and the 'Davids'. Let us look at each of these in a little more detail (and I warn you, I will be very 'frank' in this):

1. The 'Sauls'. These are the Christian leaders who have firmly aligned themselves with the present order, with its compromise, its

soulish love of 'experiences', its rejection of seeking true holiness, its love of "pleasures" more than love of God, etc. Sadly, such leaders will often welcome any new Christian fad, so long as it doesn't 'cost' them too much, and so long as it helps keep the people involved in the church. (This is why they have often welcomed new 'church growth' models and methods, etc). Beyond this, however, they stand firmly for the status quo. The thought of TRUE Reformation would absolutely horrify most of them (which is why they will oppose or persecute any genuine 'Davids' that they can identify). And when the new 'David'-type ministries arise in their church, they will often attempt to "stomp" on them, to dominate them, or if that doesn't work, to limit their influence as much as possible.

To the 'Sauls' of today's church I believe God would have me say: Because you have made yourselves "lords" over the church in Jesus' stead, God will snatch the royal scepter from your hands. And because of the compromise that has been found in your mouths for so long, God will lie much of the blame for the sickly state of today's 'lukewarm' church directly at your feet. You have been rejected by God as being unfit to lead His people. "The kingdom shall be taken from you and given unto another" (See Mt 21:43, 1 Sa 15:22-23, 1 Sa 28:17, etc). "Behold, you despisers, and wonder, and perish: for I work a work in your days, a work which you shall in no way believe, though a man declare it unto you" (Acts 13:41).

It is interesting to note that the most serious sin that Saul committed in God's eyes (the sin that finally caused him to be rejected by God as unfit to lead His people) was that after the battle with the Amelikites, Saul compromised what God had said by allowing his men to take the best of the enemy flocks as spoil, instead of killing them all. This 'men-pleasing', rebellious disregard for God's word, caused Saul to be immediately told that his kingdom would be taken from him and given to another. "For rebellion is as the sin of witchcraft, and stubbornness is as iniquity and idolatry. Because you have rejected the word of the Lord, He has also rejected you from being king" (1 Sa 15:23). Notice that it was not Saul's 'control' or domination of the people that caused him to be rejected by God, but rather his WEAKNESS AND COMPROMISE as a leader (i.e., his desire to be pleasing and 'accommodating' toward his people at the expense of God's word). Is it not the same today also?

2. The 'Jonathans'. You will no doubt remember how that Jonathan, who was Saul's son, had a tremendous devotion and love for David. They were like brothers. While Saul went about trying to kill David, Jonathan was doing his best to quietly protect and help him. I believe that there are quite a number of leaders and ministries around the world today who are just like Jonathan. They have definitely been "friends of the true Revival", but like Jonathan they are caught between their allegiance to the 'old' or existing order, and their affinity with the new ministries – the 'Davids'. They want to be part of the great Revival that God is about to send, but they are just too attached to the old system and the old ways to really let go ('compromise', again!). This is a very dangerous position to be in – in a very real way, just as dangerous as that of Saul. For it is very significant that even though Jonathan was a friend of David's (i.e., a friend of the "new move of God"), HE WAS KILLED ON THE SAME BATTLEFIELD AND ON THE SAME DAY THAT SAUL WAS KILLED. Jonathan never got to see or enter into the new move of God at all (i.e., the reign of David). In essence, HE SUFFERED EXACTLY THE SAME FATE AS SAUL.

Another thing that is significant about Jonathan was that he was the "heir apparent" (i.e., the 'obvious' choice to lead Israel in the new era, when Saul was gone). I believe that many of today's "Jonathans" are also like this. They are the seemingly 'obvious' Revival-oriented leaders of today – the kind of men who preach on Revival, prophecy and prayer, etc, but in an "acceptable" kind of way. Many of them are truly prophetic, but they fit into the current set-up just a little too well. They have a 'reputation' to uphold in the existing system, and they can be trusted not to say anything too "radical", or to rock today's "Laodicean" boat too hard. They are certainly nothing like the stench in Saul's nostrils that David was. No-one feels particularly 'threatened' by their presence.

As I have said, I believe that there are quite a number of 'Jonathans' in ministry all over the world today. The greatest danger for them is that because of their current respectability and their attachment to the existing order, they just can't imagine God bringing judgment upon the very systems and 'streams' that they have formed relationships with. They love David and all that he stands for, but they just cannot let go of Saul. Deep in their heart they are still clinging to a kind of 'acceptable' amalgam between both the existing order and also the `new move' of God (it will never happen).

Today's Jonathans would be quite happy if the 'new wine' could somehow be crammed into the old wineskins. They have their feet in both camps. And the terrible likelihood is that when the day of decision dawns, when that fateful hour arrives, because of their double-mindedness they will surely be found with Saul, rather than with David. And this can only result in tragedy. Their failure to see the signs that it is time to finally 'abandon' Saul, and throw in their lot entirely with David, means that they will surely be caught up in the very judgment that falls upon Saul. Sadly, all the signs are there that the cry, "How have the mighty fallen" is again about to ring out in our day.

To give you an idea of what God has been saying to some of the prophets in NZ about the terrible dangers of clinging to the old system, the following is a very pertinent dream that God gave to a local prophet a number of years ago:

In the dream, they found themselves standing in a grand old house that had become quite run-down, and was now in a state of decay. Running down into this house were leaking gas pipes, which were literally pumping huge volumes of highly flammable gas into the house. A man and his wife (the owners?) were inside the house also, but though they were obviously aware of the terrible danger of a huge gas explosion, THEY WERE REFUSING TO LEAVE

THE HOUSE. Suddenly the prophet was translated to a totally different building altogether, overlooking the old house. This new building was a very modern, spacious, multi-level structure, totally befitting the 1990's. The prophet was initially on the balcony on about the fourth floor, looking down on the old house, but soon felt drawn inside to a place of greater safety, KNOWING THAT THE SLIGHTEST SPARK WOULD SOON CAUSE AN EXPLOSION IN THE OLD HOUSE THAT WOULD LITERALLY TEAR IT TO PIECES. And it was at this point that the dream ended.

This dream has been confirmed by another very experienced prophet who believes that God has shown him that a time will come when the true prophets will have to strongly warn those in the churches to 'come out' and to get involved with what God is doing on the outside. I believe that this time is very near now (for the early signs of 'judgment beginning at the house of God' are already clearly visible in many churches). However, it is important that we await God's perfect timing in this 'leaving behind' of the old system. I do believe, though, that God is now calling His people to truly let go of the existing systems and ways in their hearts, in preparation for this time. We cannot afford to be found even partially clinging to 'Saul' (with his compromising, Laodicean, "experience-centered" Christianity) when that hour arrives.

3. The 'Davids'. As we have seen, by and large, the reign of King Saul was not a particularly happy time for David. However, I believe that this long, enforced period of brokenness and humility in David's life was ABSOLUTELY ESSENTIAL in preparing him to become a truly godly leader of Israel. It was at this time that David could easily have become a 'rebel', deliberately stirring up dissension against Saul in retaliation for the way he was being treated. Remember, David had already been anointed by Samuel as the future leader of Israel. He was a renowned warrior, a natural leader, a mighty man of valor. If he had wanted to, he and his men could have stirred up a great deal of trouble for Saul. But instead, with great patience and forbearance, David endured all things, treating Saul as the "Lord's anointed", respecting his authority, not

murmuring or causing dissension against him, etc. And I truly believe that we are to be like David in our attitude towards the church leaders in our own situations today.

Even though there must have been times when David felt extremely distressed, angry and hurt at Saul's treatment of him, he never allowed this to become a festering 'wound' of resentment that would cause him to "react" in rebellion against Saul. I truly believe that if David had acted out of rebellion, then he may well have proven himself to be unworthy of his calling to lead God's people. I do not believe that God ever sanctions rebellion. In fact, as we have seen, it was because of REBELLION that Saul had been rejected as king in the first place. I believe that God was watching David to make sure that this kind of rebellion was not found in him also. And of course, He is watching us for the self-same reason.

I am convinced that God would have even the 'Sauls' amongst today's Christian leaders treated as the "Lord's anointed", right up until God Himself acts to completely annul their authority, and to anoint and raise up the 'Davids' to take their place. (Please note: It is GOD who will do this, in His own perfect time). Until that time, I believe that we are to willingly give today's pastors genuine honor and loyalty as befitting God's appointed leaders over His people. We are also to GENUINELY LOVE THEM AND PRAY FOR THEM. Remember, David mourned and wept over Saul when he died. What depths of Godliness this man David had! And I firmly believe that God is calling the 'Davids' of today to be of this same spirit. We are certainly not to be like Absalom, who sat in the gates of the city some years later, murmuring and subtly turning the people to rebellion against king David. Rebellion is sin, and every one of us needs to ask God to search our hearts to see if there be any "wicked way", any dark seed of rebellion, found in us.

In saying all of this, I do not want people to think that I am advocating some kind of abject, unthinking "submission" to pastors (where you don't "think" – you just do what you are told). This is certainly not the kind of relationship that David had with Saul. In fact, while David was utterly constant in his deep love and respect for Saul, he also did his best to avoid him as much as possible, even when Saul assured him that he would be safe! David and Saul were of opposing spirits, and "how can two walk together unless they be agreed?" They were by no means real 'friends' or natural allies. This is the way it has always been between these two opposite types of leaders. One walks under God's special favor, and the other (who once knew this divine favor himself) now does not, and in their heart of hearts they both know it (which is why the 'Sauls' are so jealous).

It is also important to note that after Saul had 'died' (i.e., had his authority and anointing finally annulled by God), David was appointed as king of Judah (i.e., as the anointed and recognized leader of his own tribe). After being anointed to lead Judah, David now had no hesitation in waging war on the "house of Saul" for the leadership of the entire nation of Israel. This was no longer 'rebellion'. David was now the only rightful, God-appointed leader of the whole kingdom, and it was time for him to 'take it by force'. As the Scriptures tell us, "There was a long war between the house of Saul and the house of David; and David grew stronger and stronger, while the house of Saul became weaker and weaker" (2 Sam 3:1).

It is interesting to note the order of events that led from David as shepherd-boy to David as God-appointed leader of a united and powerful Israel (for this will essentially be the same path that many end-time 'Davids' will travel also). For David, God's first school of preparation was shepherding a small flock of sheep – an ideal training ground for later leadership. Here, David learnt to faithfully care for those he had been given charge over, and to defend them fearlessly from the ravaging 'bears and lions', etc. As Jesus said centuries later, "You have been faithful over a little, I will set you over much" (Mt 25:21).

It was now that David received his first 'kingly' anointing, by the hands of the prophet Samuel. He then burst onto the public scene in quite spectacular fashion (the victory over Goliath), but quickly found himself offside with the existing leadership, and was forced into hiding, along with his small band of outcasts. All this time, God was testing and preparing him for the great task ahead. This period of agonized "waiting" in the wilderness went on for years. Finally, with Saul 'dead', David received his second kingly anointing, and became king of Judah, from whence he waged war on the "house of Saul" for leadership of the whole nation of Israel.

David was finally anointed as leader of all Israel some years later. Under his leadership, Israel became a united, prosperous, victorious nation, mighty in battle and utterly glorifying to God – displaying His grace and glory to all nations. This is exactly what the coming move of God will bring about also. All of this is the exact purpose and reason for the coming 'Reformation' and Revival. Glory to God! And the result will be a worldwide 'harvest' of staggering proportions – a great outpouring of God's Spirit upon "all flesh", in which the knowledge of His glory will cover the earth as the waters cover the sea.

But what will be the signs that all this is fully underway? How will we be able to tell when we are to completely abandon the old compromising 'Saulish' system, and to join with the new move of God? I believe that it will not be at all difficult to recognize the signs that the 'Davids' have arisen to lead God's people out of bondage and into Revival. God will make sure that all His people are fully aware of what is occurring (though many whose hearts are still with 'Saul' will certainly not welcome the news!). This will not be a 'secret' operation. When the new Revival leaders arise, everyone will know about it. I believe that the vision recounted in chapter one, in which God fires 'flaming arrows' into the churches, gives us real insight into what is about to occur. In this particular vision, you will remember, the 'flaming arrows' that God fired into the churches were really "on-fire" ministries, speaking the word of God. The pastors ran around trying to damp down the flames, but God sent a 'mighty wind' to fan the flames, and suddenly the doors of the churches burst open, and God's people ran out onto the streets, where they all became one huge throng. It is my belief that this is exactly what is about to take place.

One of the things that I most want people to take note of in the story of David and Saul is the vital importance of WAITING FOR GOD'S PERFECT TIME AND FOR HIS ANOINTING before we move. We see this principle so clearly in the life of David. This is why I want to encourage all of you who are reading this to WAIT UNTIL GOD MOVES before you try "pulling down the old" or setting up a "New Testament"-style church, etc. It is impossible to have a true New Testament church without true New Testament APOSTLES – raised up and anointed by God. Anything that is built before these new apostles arise is almost certain to just get in their way. WE MUST AWAIT GOD'S PERFECT TIME.

I actually believe that there may be attempts by some Christians to pre-empt what God is about to do, and start a large-scale rebellious "reformation" themselves, before God's time comes. Such 'Absalom'-like rebellion will certainly not have God's blessing, and will eventually come to nothing, but for a while it may look good, and may even draw away large numbers of Christians (who will be forced to return in the end, with their tail between their legs, though a number of their leaders will never make it back). God never sanctions rebellion, and we must be aware of the difference between rebellious 'revolution' (or "coup d'état") and God-ordained "Reformation". A rebellious Absalom-type movement will tend to launch a pre-emptive strike on the existing establishment, while a true 'David'-type movement will wait until God's time has come (i.e., until Saul is 'dead' and the new anointing has arrived) before moving to assume its rightful place in leading God's people. This is a very crucial difference which may become vitally important for us to recognize in the near future. However, it is also important to realize that there are currently many signs in the church that the TRUE "shaking", Reformation and Revival are now very near – even at the doors. So let us remain alert!

THE NATURE OF TRUE AUTHORITY

In the 1970's, a teaching arose in Charismatic circles that was known as the "shepherding" teaching (or the 'covering/submission' doctrine). Unfortunately, this teaching brought in extremes that led to heavy, dominating leadership and abuse of power by a number of church leaders at that time. In the 1980's there was a "reaction" against this whole concept of 'heavy' leadership, but it seems that this reaction has also now gone too far, resulting in compromising, over-accommodating leadership in many churches. 'Soft' leadership of this kind also plays directly into the devil's hands, as history clearly shows. Surely there is a Scriptural balance to be found somewhere?

It seems fairly clear from the Bible that every aspect of ministry in the church really does involve some form of 'shepherd'-type activity. (These ministries are listed in Eph 4:11). The teacher is involved in 'feeding' God's sheep, the pastor 'shepherds', guides and cares for the flock, the evangelist specializes in 'seeking and saving' the lost or wandering sheep, the prophet is like a 'watchman', set in place to guard and warn the flock of approaching danger, etc, and the apostle holds a place of 'government', performing all of these functions put together, with miracle-working power accompanying his ministry. (The evangelist in particular should also have 'signs and wonders following'). All of these ministries work together, "For the perfecting of the saints, for the work of the ministry, for the edifying of the body of Christ: Till we all come in the unity of the faith, and of the knowledge of the Son of God, unto a perfect man, unto the MEASURE OF THE STATURE OF THE FULNESS OF CHRIST" (Eph 4:12-13).

If the Christian leaders are not "perfecting the saints" in this way, then they can eventually expect to receive 'notice' of their dismissal from their positions by God. Like any earthly employer, if His 'managers' are not performing, God reserves the right to terminate their employment and raise up others to take their place. (He has been forced to do this on quite a number of occasions down through history). God will not put up with ineffective or uninspired men leading His people for long. For, while the church is mired in a hole of its own making, the devil will be having a field-day. For the sake of the world, as well as His own people, God must have anointed, effective leaders of His Church. And if necessary, He will take drastic action to ensure that this is so, as He has done many times in the past.

It is my belief that all genuine forms of leadership ON EARTH can actually be equated with a form of 'shepherding'. Even Jesus described Himself as being the "Good Shepherd", who laid down His life for the sheep. And it is interesting to note that an important training-ground for two of His greatest leaders (David and Moses) was in shepherding sheep. But there are many other secular leadership roles which also involve the same principles. Fatherhood, for instance, was clearly seen by Paul as being good preparation for leadership in the church.

If a man was a good and effective father and husband, then this was taken as a sign of His potential in leading God's people. In fact, Paul encouraged those who were evaluating men for eldership to look at their children (the 'fruit' of their leadership in the home): "He must manage his own household well, keeping his children submissive and respectful in every way; for if a man does not know how to manage his own household, how can he care for God's church?" (1 Tim 3:4-5). It is obvious from this and other passages that there are strong similarities between the leadership required in being a 'shepherd' of God's people and also in being 'shepherd' of a family. With a family, a father must be strong and willing to bring correction where necessary, but he must also be loving and patient. If a father abuses his power by becoming a 'heavy', unloving, harsh "dictator in the home", then his wife and children will suffer real emotional, psychological (and often physical) damage that may affect them for years. On the other hand, if the father's authority and discipline are effectively 'absent' from the home (either through being overly 'soft' and "eager-to-please", or through being physically absent), then his children may become rebellious and scornful of authority. (The children will often grow up not respecting either him, their school-teachers or other authority figures).

True, godly fatherhood involves both authoritative discipline, along with true patience and love. We must have a balance of both. In these "politically-correct" times, today's men are often made to feel guilty if they wish to establish their rightful place as 'head of the house'. This is simply ridiculous "New Age" garbage (RENOUNCE IT!). Much of the disastrous mess in today's Western society can be traced directly back to the rise of these modern, so-called "liberating" philosophies. God has ordained that men are to be 'head of the house', and if this and other authority bench-marks are tampered with, then society rapidly becomes a disaster-zone of lawlessness and rebellion.

Today, we are paying a colossal price for the permissiveness of recent decades. In many modern homes, it is the television that rules the household, dictating the 'times and seasons' of the entire family, with the 'sensitive, New Age' parents surrendering much of their influence and authority to a 'box' in the corner. At other times, we find wives skillfully manipulating their rather pathetic 'New Age' husbands ('Jezebel' again). Tell me, when will the REAL MEN stand up and say "ENOUGH!"? (Of course, it is the same in the church today also. Permissive leadership is 'in' and Jezebel rules supreme. Only true, godly authority can ever rectify this situation).

It is interesting to note that almost all of the new "liberation" philosophies that arose in the late sixties were aimed at undermining or attacking basic moral or authority structures, etc. Many of them also attacked the position of 'men' in society. The sexual revolution, the feminist movement, the "anti-disciplining of children" movement, etc, have all had a profound effect on Western culture. Men have lost much of their responsibility, their authority, their rightful position in society and their right to enforce that position. They stand confused and ashamed under the barrage of general condemnation of their sex, and their natural place in the world. Many men have believed these lies (that all men are "abusers of power", etc), and have even cooperated in allowing their sex to be essentially dethroned and emasculated.

Whose work does all this sound like to you? As history clearly shows, the devil is a great student of the "bind the strongman" principle. He understands very well the statement that Jesus made about "binding the strongman of the house so that you can spoil his goods." (See Mt 12:29). We are told that the devil came to "kill and steal and destroy". The way he does this is often by first binding, deceiving or removing those who are in authority, and then 'spoiling' all that is in their domain. This applies to both secular and spiritual situations, and the devil has used it time and time again, to great effect. Why do you think the devil is able to captivate and destroy this present generation far more than the generation of 40 years ago? What has changed? Simply this: Many of the 'strongmen' (the sources of true authority, both small and great) in our society have been 'bound', and the devil is now 'spoiling' all that was once under their domain.

Like much that is happening in today's church, the whole sixties party culture and "liberty revolution" scenario truly reek of 'Jezebel'. All the signs of her handiwork are there. She loves to create and exploit a vacuum of true authority and leadership. She has already done so in the secular world, as we have just seen, and now she is doing so on an unprecedented scale in the church. However, "When the enemy comes in like a flood, the Spirit of the Lord shall lift up a standard..." (Is 59:19). Because the spirit of Jezebel has arisen with such great power in recent years, we can now begin to expect God to once again raise up the only ministries that can ever truly combat and defeat her: the Elijah ministries. The signs are now everywhere that the end-times 'Elijahs' are truly about to arise (because they are now so desperately needed!). When they do, they will expose and destroy Jezebel's every stronghold, first in the church and then in the world. This is what "taking the kingdom by force" is all about.

In many ways, the over-riding theme of Jezebel's handiwork could be summed up in one word: "REBELLION". She constantly works to undermine or destroy all forms of authority (including God-given instincts, basic morality and even "common sense"). She loves to 'thumb her nose at God' and cause others to do likewise, by leading them into rebellion against any form of true authority. Thus, "casting off restraint", rejecting or undermining true 'authorities' (Scriptures, parents, leaders, morals, the law, etc), the casting off of natural inhibitions or accepted "norms" of behavior, wild or abandoned 'partying' (which is an integral part of many pagan religions) – these are all just part of Jezebel's stock-in-trade.

Rebellion can take many forms, from simple mocking disregard for the authority of parents through to the overthrowing of basic, instinctive moral restraints in society ("Gay Liberation", etc – such movements are just steeped in rebellion). It is noticeable that Jezebel often causes those under her sway to openly mock authority figures. Her favorite activities involve causing men and women to blatantly or gleefully parade their "casting off of restraint" right before God's very eyes, so to speak. This is why control of the church is Jezebel's most coveted prize – she loves the thought of leading God's people into some kind of open lawlessness or 'casting off restraint'. And it is always through the church leaders that she will seek to establish her control (for she cannot move unless the leaders give her 'room').

As I said before, the devil and his demons are well aware of the "bind the strongman and spoil his goods" principle. This is why, when they are trying to deceive or destroy a movement, they will often primarily target the leaders. If the main leader (or leaders) can somehow be taken out, or made to fall into sin or deception, then the whole movement can often be either "hijacked" for the devil's purposes, or else completely destroyed. How many times have we seen this "strike the shepherd and the sheep will scatter" principle apply to situations in today's church? Whole movements (sometimes very promising ones) have been crippled by the devil in this way, even in recent times. And the same principle applies, from tiny groups (i.e., families), right up to whole nations and movements: Target the main leaders, bind (with sin and compromise) the 'strongman' of the house and spoil his goods. (Kill, steal and destroy his "children", etc).

However, if the 'strongman' of the house will not compromise – if he makes his stand, using all the authority that is rightfully his as leader or parent, then the devil will find it very difficult to get in. This is why God has spent so much time training and preparing the leaders of the coming move of God.

I BELIEVE IN LEADERS!

Something I want to establish very strongly here is that the coming new leaders must NEVER BE AFRAID TO TRULY "LEAD" GOD'S PEOPLE. If God appoints them to lead, then let them LEAD!

Over the last ten years or so, I have often moved in circles in which it has been emphasized that any future Revival must have "no superstars and no personalities". Sounds good! Obviously, all the glory must go to God, and self-promotion, pride and the idolizing of human leadership must have no place. But very often, I have found that this whole "no superstars, no personalities" thing has been taken much further, into the realm of basically desiring that there be no prominent leaders at all. So what do we really mean by all this? Do we mean to say that God is now finished with "men of valor" and men of 'renown' – the Joshuas, the Gideons and the Davids of ages past? Are we really now to have a kind of "leaderless" Revival, as some have stated? (Declaring that God has little need for prominent leaders at all, and that He Himself will do all the leading, with almost no requirement for earthly 'shepherds'). Sounds so right, doesn't it? So "spiritual" – so democratic. No superstars and no personalities. You have to admit, it has a nice ring to it.

The only problem is if you take this concept to its logical conclusion, then you have to do away with almost every major form of ministry found in the Bible. If God had operated this way in the past, then there would never have been a Moses or a Joshua, a Gideon or a Sampson, a Samuel or an Elijah, a David or a John-the-Baptist, a Peter or a Paul, a Martin Luther or a John Wesley, a

William Booth or a Charles Finney (etc, etc, etc...). No heroes, no leaders, no apostles, no "mighty men" of valor or renown to lead God's people into war. For what use does God have of such men, when He can lead the people Himself? All of the men we have just mentioned were God's "heroes" of their day – men whom God had raised up into a place of prominence and renown to lead His people, usually after secretly training them for years in the 'wilderness'. And it has to be said: Every one of them was a strong and authoritative type of leader (because that is exactly what God had raised them up to be).

For me personally, this whole question has been one that I have pondered at length over the last few years. And I have to admit that during that time, what God has shown me has caused me to adopt the exact opposite position to that which I formerly held. I can no longer believe in a "leaderless" Revival. Everything that I have ever read about past moves of God, from the beginning of the Old Testament right down through recent Revival history has convinced me that this whole "leaderless" concept is a dangerous and deceptive fallacy. Not only is it almost entirely lacking in reason or historical legitimacy, but it actually goes against the very character of God and His dealings with men right down through the ages. For God has ALWAYS USED MEN AND WOMEN as His instruments to bring repentance, deliverance or Revival to His people and as carriers of His anointing - displaying His glory to a dying world. And He has always raised up STRONG LEADERS to establish and carry forward almost every new move that He has visited upon the earth. I am convinced that He is about to do so again, in the coming great Revival.

A true Revival leader must never be 'soft' or compromising, but neither must he be harsh or authoritarian. He must be both a strong and a loving man of God – wise, patient, "apt to teach", but also not afraid to "reprove, rebuke and exhort" where necessary. Above all else, in these mild and insipid times, HE MUST NOT BE AFRAID TO BE A TRUE 'LEADER', despite what people say. History clearly demonstrates that with an 'absence' of strong leadership, the devil gets in so fast that the coming Revival would probably only last a matter of months (if that).

What happened to the 1904 Welsh Revival after Evan Roberts (who was without a doubt one of God's great Revivalists) suddenly disappeared from the scene, should be an object lesson to us all. Within a very short space of time after he was gone, the whole Revival was being absolutely taken apart by the enemy, with no-one else around with the overall authority to correct the excesses, expose the counterfeits or keep the whole thing on the rails. It seems that Evan Roberts (whose Revival preaching was being reported by secular newspapers around the world at that time) had been persuaded by certain parties that his prominence in the Revival was somehow "stealing glory away from God". So, as a truly humble man, he took what he obviously thought was the most 'humble' or "spiritual" option available – he hid himself away in a small house, and refused to see anyone or to preach again for many years.

Thus, with GOD'S true "strongman" gone (the one man with the true mantle and anointing, raised up by God to lead the Revival), the devil now had free reign to 'spoil his goods'. In many ways this disaster could be likened to the children of Israel suddenly losing Moses after crossing the Red Sea, or losing Joshua just as they entered the Promised Land. The result was entirely predictable. Chaos! The devil had an absolute field-day, and the famous Welsh Revival, which should have been one of God's enduring victories, ended in relative ignominy after little more than one year. Excesses and counterfeits flooded in, and thousands of young converts fell away (though many thousands still remained, and some new Pentecostal groups were able to emerge – so not all was lost).

I hope I am not being ungracious to the memory of one of God's greatest Revivalists here. Please believe me, I hold Evan Roberts in the highest regard. But I believe it is very important that we learn the lessons from this, and other moves of God down through history. The simple fact of the matter is: NO LEADERS – NO REVIVAL. If those whom God is calling to be leaders of a new move of God fail to truly "LEAD" it, then the devil is able to very easily undermine or destroy what God is doing. It is not "humble" to refuse to take authority and be a strong leader when God is calling you to do so – It is simply irresponsible and disobedient. And the same will be true of the coming move of God also. This is the exact reason why God is about to raise up so many currently hidden "men of authority" (apostles and prophets...) as leaders of the coming great move.

The Revivals under Luther, Wesley and Booth were also quite significant in this regard. They were not perfect, but at least the leaders recognized the need for constant, authoritative leadership. This is no doubt one reason why these particular Revivals lasted as long as they did. (Another reason is that they were 'outward looking' – taking the Revival anointing out onto the streets – especially Wesley and Booth. They also had a 'new wineskin' – new leaders, new structures, etc. All of these things were key factors).

The coming Revival will need strong leaders right from the start. And no doubt God has a hidden supply of these (as always), ready to take the field at His command. Glory to God! I also believe that in the coming move, new converts will grow up and fulfill their potential in God very rapidly. New ministries will arise and mature at a startling rate. God will raise up both the very young and the very old. After all, isn't this maturing of new, vigorous, anointed ministries one of the very reasons why God appoints leaders in His church (to bring them to maturity)? True leadership of God's flock has clearly always been a great privilege, but also an awesome responsibility.

UNDERSTANDING TRUE AUTHORITY

I am absolutely convinced that this issue of "godly authority" and the believer's exercise of it is actually central to the entire coming Revival. (After all, the apostles COMMANDED people to be healed in Jesus' name, etc). The whole concept of being given the authority and the anointing by God to be able to subdue a particular 'kingdom' in His name, to 'take it by force' and establish God's reign there (as Joshua did with the promised land) is vital to fully comprehending God's purposes for the coming move. This whole concept of 'taking the kingdom by force' and maintaining His rule there, is to be applied, not only on a large scale, but also firstly in our own personal lives. The coming Revival ministries will have a very deep understanding of what it means to walk fully in such God-given authority – using His anointed 'word' to establish His kingdom in any given situation. (As I have said before, God's 'kingdom' is any place where enemy ruler-ship has been overthrown, and where "God's will is now done"). The new ministries won't need to 'strive' to somehow manufacture this anointed word. They will simply walk in this authority as a "normal" state.

As Jesus said: "For the Son of Man is as a man taking a far journey, who left his house, and gave AUTHORITY to his servants..." (Mk 13:34). "Behold, I give you power to tread on serpents and scorpions, and OVER ALL THE POWER OF THE ENEMY (Lk 10:19). "Heal the sick, cleanse the lepers, RAISE THE DEAD, cast out demons. Freely you have received, freely give..." (Mt 10:8). "He that believes on me, the works that I do he shall do also, and GREATER WORKS THAN THESE shall he do" (Jn 14:12). Of course, such authority can only ever function safely if it is in total submission to God. This is why God must spend years training and 'breaking' His servants before He can ever entrust them with such power.

The mighty apostles, prophets and evangelists, etc, that are about to arise will truly walk in the resurrection glory of Jesus Christ. Here is how the apostle John described the risen, glorified Christ: "His head and His hair were white like wool, as white as snow, and His eyes were as a flame of fire. His feet were like fine brass, as if they burned in a furnace, and His voice as the sound of many waters. He had in His right hand seven stars, and out of His mouth went a sharp, two-edged sword. And His face was as the sun shining in its strength. And when I saw Him, I fell at His feet, as dead" (Rev 1:14-17). This is the Jesus whose glory will be openly displayed for all to see by the mightily-anointed "street-church" of tomorrow. This is the Jesus who baptizes "with the Holy Spirit AND WITH FIRE". This is the Jesus who is truly worthy of all honor, praise and glory, in heaven and on earth.

I can no longer believe in a church that does not openly glorify Jesus Christ on the streets of every city. I cannot believe in a church that is so bereft of the genuine MIRACLE-working power of God, as that which we call the "church" today. Where are the Elijahs of God? Why do we seem so satisfied merely to watch as the world goes to hell all around us? I can frankly no longer believe in a "church" in which Jesus lies 'wounded in the house of His friends'.

The Church I believe in is an invading force, a rampaging army that cuts a swathe over the whole earth, "destroying the works of the devil". It is a people of great power and ruthless determination, who batter down every 'gate' of hell and utterly destroy every stronghold, so that the oppressed might be liberated and the captives be set free. This will be a 'Joshua' army, commissioned by God to "take the land", to raze every work of Satan to the ground and slaughter every living thing in the enemy camp. Like Jesus, they will 'set their faces as flint' toward the Holy City, and nothing will stand in their path.

In saying all of this, however, I do want to make it clear that I am not speaking here of "taking over" the earth's political and educational systems, etc. This teaching (which is known as 'dominion theology') is quite widespread in some circles. However, the war that I am talking about is an entirely "SPIRITUAL" one – a war for the hearts and the minds of men. It is certainly not a war for control of the world's secular institutions (for, as Jesus clearly stated, "My kingdom is not of this world" – Jn 18:36). The purpose of the battle that is about to be waged will be to expose and destroy the lies that bind the people of the earth, and to bring down the 'principalities and powers' that hold them captive. Destroying every 'work' and stronghold of the devil – that's what this is all about.

THE REFINING OF THE 'DAVIDS'

In closing this chapter, I would just like to return briefly to our analogy of the Sauls, the Jonathans and the Davids. There can be no doubt that God has been preparing a "David company" of leaders to arise and lead His people into the coming Revival – leaders after His own heart who have been in hidden preparation for years. However, a large number of these 'David'-type ministries will probably have been badly stung by some of their dealings with the present 'Saulish' system. As I have said, the 'Davids' will almost always feel like misfits in the current church set-up. They are essentially 'designed' to fit into the revived church of tomorrow rather than the Laodicean church of today.

Some of them will have received such a hammering whenever they have dared to speak up in the past, that they have now become quite 'crushed' and hesitant about sharing their convictions. Others will be feeling rather 'lonely' – wondering if they are the only ones in their church who feel the way they do about the state of things. There will be others again who, like David, have felt compelled to withdraw from the current system altogether, to a place of refuge far away from the 'Sauls'. Still others may have felt called into the 'wilderness', just so that they can spend time alone with God, learning from Him. Believe me, I can sympathize with all of these. However, I also believe that it is extremely vital that the Davids deal with any hurts, resentments, bitterness, rejection, or rebellion that have found a place in their hearts due to their unhappy dealings with the churches, or other 'authorities'. Not only is this vitally important, but it is also URGENT I believe, because God is going to want to use these 'David' ministries in a great way very soon. For if the refining process is not complete, how can they hope to be a part of what God is about to do?

Every one of us needs to search our hearts to make sure that there is no deep root of resentment or rebellion lurking within us, as a result of our past dealings with authority figures (pastors, parents, etc), or other Christians. We need to be extremely thorough and totally honest with ourselves. We must not make excuses. We must deal with the root of the problem. Past wounds and resentments, etc, can have a tremendous effect on our present attitudes towards authority. These kinds of bad experiences can cause us to become "reactionary" – still reacting against these wounds many years later. This is often the source of 'rebellion' in many peoples' hearts. If we are 'prophetic', then such wounds will almost certainly harshly distort many of our prophetic words. (In fact, it has been truly said that many false prophets are really true prophets with 'unhealed wounds'). It is vital that we search our hearts, and deal with these deep 'roots' or strongholds in our lives as urgently as possible (for they can seep poison right through every part of our lives, if we are not careful).

Here are some sure signs of 'rebellion' in a person's life: They secretly enjoy hearing or seeing authority figures or institutions mocked or made a fool of. They can't seem to help 'murmuring' or complaining to others against particular authority figures that they know. They enjoy deliberately speaking or acting (or even dressing) in such a way that will shock the "establishment". (MOTIVES are the things that need to be looked at here). This list could go on and on, but I am sure you get the idea; "REBELLION" – a truly subtle yet deadly sin (and one of Satan's all-time favorites).

How do we deal with such 'roots' of rebellion deep within us? In exactly the same way as we deal with roots or strongholds of any other kind: We ask God to shed light on them, and then utterly 'RENOUNCE' them in the name of Jesus Christ, not just with our words, but also from the depths of our very being. With rebellion, it will also often be necessary to ask God's forgiveness and cleansing (with genuine godly sorrow). One thing that true godly sorrow and deep repentance will always produce is a genuine HATRED OF SIN, and this will bring abundant 'good fruit' into our lives.

As I said before, honoring and respecting authority does not necessarily mean abject, unthinking "submission" towards our leaders. We are still all individually responsible for our own walk before God, and we need to be sure that our leaders are not leading us astray. If they are leading us into serious deception, then God will often expect us to make a stand and say something about it. If this is done in the right spirit, then it is certainly not 'rebellion'. However, if the deception continues, then after making our stand known, the best thing to do would probably be to leave that particular group (unless God tells us to stay). We are not to be unthinking 'slaves' to authority, but neither are we to ever be found amongst the rebellious "murmurers and complainers". God will help us judge what is right, if our hearts are pure before him. We are certainly not obliged to be loyal to any man who is leading us into blatant deception. Really, I guess the best policy always is "BALANCE IN ALL THINGS".

Just a short word here about the (often young) harsh, immature 'prophet'-types who go around "blasting" people with bludgeoning, judgmental prophecies, etc (I used to be one of these myself, some years ago!). Often, such 'prophets' may have a true calling on their life, but their immaturity, their (unknowing) pride and arrogance, and their secret 'rebellion' make them very dangerous to themselves and to others. Until they allow God to bring true brokenness and humility into their lives (an often painful process), then they will usually end up causing more harm than good wherever they go. There is a time for 'rebuking' (though only experienced ministries should ever really consider it), but most of the time, there is no substitute for "speaking the truth in love". Wisdom, patience, gentleness meekness and love should all be part of the 'strength' that God has built into our ministries. Otherwise we can end up doing great damage to His precious flock. (For words can inflict great harm). Please think and pray about these things?

Chapter Six

TWO REVIVALS?

In recent times the movement known as the "Toronto Blessing" and similar movements have swept through many churches worldwide, particularly in the Western nations. These movements have brought with them some rather 'strange' spiritual manifestations which have caused quite a bit of controversy in the church. The purpose of this chapter is to examine the FACTS and the historical data related to this issue, in as straight-forward a way as possible. As stated earlier, I have been studying Revival and Reformation history now for many years, and I hope that this will help me to provide an informed and factual perspective.

As is now well-known, the Toronto Airport Vineyard church (home of the 'Toronto Blessing') was finally expelled from the international Vineyard movement in December 1995. This expulsion came after what had apparently been twelve months of repeated warnings given to the Toronto church by John Wimber and the Vineyard Association.

I have to say on a personal level, before going any further, that having witnessed the 'Toronto' phenomena for myself, and having spoken to many people who have experienced it, right from the outset I have personally been deeply disturbed by much of what I have seen and heard. However, it is time now to take a look at what history has to say about such phenomena.

As many who have studied Revivals will know, it is important to remember that not only have there been many genuine Revivals down through history, but also many "counterfeit" movements as well (a number of which have resulted in quasi-'Christian' cults that are still with us today). Even some of the most powerful true Revivals have eventually been infiltrated (or in some cases 'hijacked') through the devil flooding them with excesses and demonic manifestations, etc. Many of the great Revivalists came across such counterfeits on a regular basis, and wrote warnings against them. As John Wesley said: "At the first, revival is true and pure, but after a few weeks watch for counterfeits." These false or demonic manifestations have often followed a very distinctive pattern. And alarmingly, I have to say that they have often resembled 'Toronto' very closely indeed (as we shall see).

The following is an extract from a century-old book by T.W. Caskey, in which he recalls many of the religious happenings in the southern states of America in the early 1800's. This was the period when many huge 'Camp Meetings' were held in the South, accompanied by great religious excitement (which they called 'revival'): "Some would fall prostrate and lie helpless for hours at a time... The whole congregation by some inexplicable nervous action would sometimes be thrown into side-splitting convulsions of laughter and when it started, no power could check or control it until it ran its course. At other times the nervous excitement set the muscles to twitching and jerking at a fearful rate and finally settle down to regular, straight-forward dancing. Like the 'Holy Laugh' it was simply ungovernable until it ran its course. When a man started laughing, dancing, shouting or jerking, it was impossible for him to stop until exhausted nature broke down in a death-like swoon..." The same writer goes on to tell how eventually a few preachers began to question whether such excitement really was the work of the Holy Spirit. Gradually, people began to 'search the Scriptures' and 'test the spirits' a lot more than they had been, and these rather 'bizarre' manifestations began to die out.

Another historian has written of the great Camp Meetings of the eighteenth century (particularly those in Kentucky), that crowds would often "go into trances, writhe on the ground and even bark like dogs". As is well-known to many who have studied Revivals, such counterfeits and excesses have often flooded in particularly towards the end of a true Revival, when the devil has been trying to get in and completely destroy or discredit it. This is precisely what happened with the 1904 Welsh Revival (as you will see if you read "War on the Saints" by Jessie Penn-Lewis and Evan Roberts – a disturbing book which probably places too much emphasis on the devil, but vividly describes many counterfeit manifestations very similar to what we are seeing today. Such counterfeits are also examined in Watchman Nee's "The Spiritual Man").

A number of 'Toronto' writers have implied that many old-time Revivalists such as John Wesley, Charles Finney and Jonathan Edwards would be very happy with such manifestations. This is far from the truth. I have studied the lives of these men, and all of them were strong "REPENTANCE" preachers who were very suspicious of any 'bizarre' goings-on. When people fell down in their meetings it was almost always under tremendous distress and CONVICTION OF SIN. This is very different from Toronto.

The great Revivalist John Wesley, who came across many examples of counterfeit manifestations in his years of Revival ministry, wrote of one particular occasion: "God suffered Satan to teach them better. Both of them were suddenly seized in the same manner as the rest, and laughed whether they would or no, almost without ceasing. This they continued for two days, a spectacle to all; and were then, upon prayer being made for them, delivered in a moment." Charles Finney wrote, concerning the dangers of simply 'yielding' to strange impulses or impressions: "God's Spirit leads men by the intelligence, not through mere impressions... I have known some cases where persons have rendered themselves highly ridiculous, have greatly injured their own souls, and the cause of God, by giving themselves up to an enthusiastic and fanatical following of impressions."

And Jonathan Edwards wrote, concerning the supposedly 'heavenly' trances that members of his congregation were entering into under the ministry of Samuel Buelle (a visiting preacher): "But when the people were raised to this height, Satan took the advantage, and his interposition in many instances soon became very apparent; and a great deal of caution and pains were found necessary to keep the people, many of them from running wild."

As Frank Bartleman (of the 1906 'Azusa Street' Revival said: "Many are willing to seek 'power' from every battery they can lay their hands on, in order to perform miracles... A true 'Pentecost' will produce a mighty conviction for sin, a turning to God. False manifestations produce only excitement and wonder... Any work that exalts the Holy Ghost or the 'gifts' above Jesus will finally land up in fanaticism." Does it sound like these men welcomed 'bizarre' manifestations to you? Certainly not! They knew how to discern what was of God and what was not.

In mid-1995, respected international Bible Teacher Derek Prince put out a tape in which he made some very strong statements about certain aspects of the Toronto movement. Like him, I would like to state categorically that I believe that human beings manifesting animal noises or animal behaviour is not of God, but rather of the devil. (In fact, he described on the tape how he had seen many such animal manifestations during demonic rituals he had witnessed in Africa). And what about the bodily distortions and the 'jerking' that have also become associated with today's 'Toronto' movement? Is it God who desires to distort the bodies of His people so that they look like sufferers of Cerebral Palsy, Epilepsy, Parkinson's Disease, etc? (Repetitive 'jerking' is also seen regularly in many mental hospitals – ask any psychiatric nurse). I have to ask the question here: Whose work does all this sound like to you?

Alarmingly, there are also many exact similarities between the Toronto experience and the demonic manifestations found throughout the New Age movement and also many pagan religions. A number of Indian gurus such as Bagwhan Shree Rajneesh and Ramakrishna have had the power to transfer a state of rapturous bliss to their followers merely by touching them. In the case of Ramakrishna, these states could last from a few minutes to several days, and were often accompanied by uncontrollable laughter or weeping. Swami Baba Muktananda also had this power, according to a former devotee, and the resulting 'Kundalini' manifestations included uncontrollable laughing, roaring, barking, crying, shaking, etc. Some of his followers also became mute or unconscious, while many felt themselves infused with feelings of tremendous joy, peace and love.

All such experiences have been based on "yielding" oneself to the power working through these gurus. Is it any coincidence that the manifestations associated with these demonic 'Kundalini' cults are almost identical to those of Toronto? Could it be that the same 'spirits' are at work? When Yan Xin, a Chinese 'Qigong' spiritual Master, gave a talk to a crowd in San Francisco in 1991, the San Francisco Chronicle reported that many in the crowd began to experience what Yan called "spontaneous movements". He told his audience, "Those who are sensitive might start having some strong physical sensations – or start laughing or crying. Don't worry. This is quite normal." Likewise, the demonic "ministry" of renowned eighteenth-century occultic healer Franz Mesmer, was also known to produce many similar manifestations (falling down, jerking, convulsions, strange grunts and cries, hysterical laughter, etc).

To me, it seems beyond dispute that there has been a powerful alien spirit let loose in many churches for some considerable time. The kind of manifestations that we have been discussing do not belong in true Christianity at all, and never have. They are completely unsupportable from the Scriptures. Many Christians seem to think that if they are receiving their teaching in a church building, then they are quite safe from deception. But I am afraid the Bible does not support this point of view at all. Just because the Toronto manifestations have been cloaked in "Christian" terminology does not mean that they are from God. The fact is that such manifestations are found nowhere in the Bible, but rather right through the New Age movement. Shouldn't this fact alone have rung alarm bells? Personally, I have been utterly astonished that such a movement could sweep through the churches with such ease. Surely if these are the 'last days' – the days of "great deception" and 'lying signs and wonders' – then we ought to be a little more careful about what we introduce into God's church?

It is my strong belief that the whole 'Toronto' affair has been a very powerful "test" that God has deliberately allowed to come upon

His church. After all, He has allowed similar times of trial and testing to come upon His people in the past, especially when He was about to move again in a great way. One important example of this, of course, was the time of testing that He put the children of Israel through in the wilderness, just before they reached the promised land. And tragically, only a tiny remnant – the two families of Joshua and Caleb – survived to enter Canaan from out of that entire generation. The rest were overthrown by God in the wilderness. Even the great leader Moses was unable to enter in.

Many Christians who have become involved with Toronto have obviously assumed that it "must be of God" because it often results in 'inner healing' or other spiritual experiences. However, such occurrences are certainly not conclusive proof that this movement is of God. In fact, the devil specializes in providing virtually identical experiences in occult and New Age groups right around the world. And as is well-known, "inner healing" has always been one of the very major emphases of today's New Age movement (while it cannot be found in the Bible). Such experiences are obviously something that Satan finds it very easy to manufacture, especially when he is given the opportunity on such a grand scale. As the Bible clearly states, the devil will gladly disguise himself as an "angel of light" in order to deceive Christians (2 Cor 11:14).

One of the most dangerous and obviously "New Age" aspects of Toronto has been the emphasis on 'switching off your mind', getting your mind "out of the way", yielding yourself unthinkingly to the spirit that is operating, etc. I tell you, this exact practice is used all over the world to open up New Age devotees to demonic influence. It is literally the most dangerous, the most deadly practice that I have ever heard taught to Christians. It plays right into the devil's hands.

The Bible makes it very clear that many demonic spirits are well capable of masquerading as the "Holy Spirit". This is why the apostle John wrote: "Beloved, do not believe every spirit, but test the spirits to see whether they are of God" (1 Jn 4:1). I am afraid I cannot agree with the idea of 'directing' the Holy Spirit, or proclaiming, "Come, Holy Spirit!" To me, such unscriptural practices are bound to lead to deception sooner or later. But the concept of just "switching off your mind" and yielding to whatever spiritual impulses come upon you, surely has to be the most dangerous teaching of all.

As Jessie Penn-Lewis wrote (in conjunction with Welsh Revival leader Evan Roberts): "... these demons hover round the soul, and make strange suggestions to the mind of something odd, or outlandish, or contrary to common sense or decent taste. They make these suggestions under the profession of being the Holy Ghost. They fan the emotions, and produce a strange, fictitious exhilaration, which is simply their bait to get into some faculty of the soul... another person said he felt like rolling on the floor, and groaning and pulling the chairs around, but he distinctly perceived that the impulse to do so had something wild in it; and a touch of self display contrary to the gentleness and sweetness of Jesus; and, as quick as he saw it was an attack of a false spirit, he was delivered. But another man had the same impulse, and fell down groaning and roaring, beating the floor with his hands and feet, and the demon entered into him as an angel of light, and got him to think that his conduct was of the Holy Ghost, and it became a regular habit in the meetings he attended, until he would ruin every religious meeting he was in... The effects of being influenced by this sort of demon is manifold, and plainly legible to a well-poised mind. They cause people to run off into things that are odd and foolish, unreasonable and indecent..."

The above authors also make the following very crucial statement in the same book: "The false conception of 'surrender' as yielding the body to supernatural power, with the mind ceasing to act, is the HIGHEST SUBTLETY OF THE ENEMY". Surely, no-one who is reading this can still be in any doubt as to what spiritual 'source' the Toronto movement is from?

It is well-known throughout Christendom that the Bible speaks of the 'last days' as being a time of great deception and apostasy. Jesus Himself said of the 'last days' that many deceivers would come "in His name" and would lead many astray (Mt 24:5). He also stated that the deceptions that would arise in the end times would be so powerful that if it were possible, even the "very elect" would be deceived (Mt 24:24).

The apostle Paul was also full of warnings about this period: "... in the last days PERILOUS TIMES WILL COME. For men shall be lovers of their own selves... lovers of pleasures more than lovers of God" (2 Tim 3:1-4). "For the time will come when they will not endure sound doctrine; but after their own lusts shall they heap to themselves teachers, having ITCHING EARS; And they shall turn away their ears from the truth, and shall be turned unto FABLES" (2 Tim 4:3-4). "Now the Spirit speaks expressly that in the latter times some shall depart from the faith, giving heed to SEDUCING SPIRITS, and doctrines of devils" (1 Tim 4:1).

There have been several dreams and visions given to New Zealand prophets and intercessors about the Toronto Movement. In one particularly powerful dream given to an Auckland man many months before the term "Toronto Blessing" was even heard of here, he was shown that there would be TWO revivals. (This was the same man who was also given the open vision of the Bride of Christ described in Chapter One). In this dream of the "TWO REVIVALS", he found himself in a large auditorium full of people. He noticed that many of those down the front of the meeting (particularly those who looked large and spiritually 'fat') were FALLING DOWN LAUGHING AND CRYING, etc. The words that were clearly spoken to him to describe what he was seeing were: "LAODICEAN REVIVAL". He was then taken and seated with the 'little' people in the auditorium, who had not become really "caught up" in this falling and laughing, etc. (though some had experienced a bit of it). As the prophet sat with them, these 'little' people were steadily drawn away from this "Laodicean" scenario, until there was a yawning gulf between them and those who were still 'partying on' at the front of the hall. Suddenly, thousands of young people burst out all around them, and they began to minister to them in the name of the Lord Jesus

Christ. The prophet knew that this was the beginning of the true Revival. Glory to God!

It is my belief that in many ways the Toronto experience has been the perfect deception for today's Laodicean church: It cost nothing, it was "instant" and convenient, it conferred spiritual blessings, 'touches' and experiences without any need for conviction of sin, deep repentance or 'taking up the cross', and best-of-all it gave a flagging, powerless church some new 'signs' to prove that "all was well" after all. The real issue that lies at the heart of this whole controversy is one that revolves around the very character of God Himself. For it is obvious that we have been asked to choose between at least two "Gods" here.

On the one hand we have Toronto's version of "God" – a being who lives to bring 'touches' and bodily sensations upon his people, and who loves to "party" with them – to 'loosen them up' so that they cast off all restraint and do foolish things that they would never normally do. Many of these 'touches' may appear to outside observers to be 'ugly' or even revolting and frightening (similar to asylum-type mental or drug disorders, etc), but, hey, let's just get our mind "out of the way", relax and enjoy it all! Who cares if it looks or sounds completely 'demonic' (animal noises, hysterical laughter, bizarre jerking, etc), so long as it feels good and seems to heal all those past 'hurts'? To me, this is the very essence of the touchy-feely "Laodicean" view of God – a 'God' made entirely in their own image, and for their own convenience. Love without responsibility. Mercy without judgement. A permissive "Santa Claus" God – perfect for the shallow, pleasure-loving age in which we live.

On the other hand, there is the God of the Bible: Yes, He is a God of love, but also of justice and of judgment. Yes, He is a God of mercy, but also of war and of vengeance – waiting patiently for the hour when His enemies will be delivered into His hand, so that He can cast them forever into a living hell. Yes, He is a God of liberty, but He is also a jealous God, who visits the sins of the fathers onto the third and fourth generation of those who hate Him. Yes, He is a

God of compassion, but He is also a God of glorious majesty, might and power. And above all, He is a God of HOLINESS, who HATES SIN so much that He created a lake of fire in which to imprison all who have given themselves over to it. And I tell you now, He is not a God who could in any way be represented by a movement involving animal behavior, animal grunts and cries, drunken stupidity, insane laughter, or ugly epileptic-type 'jerking' amongst His people. Anyone who believes that God may be represented by such sick and ridiculous ugliness is frankly worshipping the wrong God, or does not truly know the Living God at all.

This is why Toronto was such a good 'test' for the Laodicean church. It was a test to see who truly does "know their God". And how do you think He feels about all those thousands of Christians around the world who chose to give themselves over to a false "God" and a counterfeit spirit – who didn't even know Him well enough to recognize the difference? And what of those who led them into it? It is my belief that this 'Laodicean revival' has exposed the lukewarm church for what she really is – a "sitting duck", almost completely prone to the most obvious deception from the enemy – a "happiness club", still desperate for feel-good 'touches' and blessings after all these years.

It is significant to note that many of the parables that Jesus told about the last days speak of the people of God being 'sifted' and "separated" (for instance, the parables of the 'tares and the wheat' and the 'wise and foolish virgins', etc). Is it not possible that God might use something like the recent deception to begin this sifting and separating of His people? The Bible makes it clear that judgment is to begin "at the house of God" (1 Pe 4:17). And it is a fact that the Greek word for 'judgment' used in the Bible usually involves 'a separating or categorizing'. Thus, in the parables of the 'sheep and the goats' and the 'tares and the wheat' for instance, we see the people being separated into two distinct groups or 'categories' as part of the judgment process. Whether it is "deception" in the last days that will bring about this separation in the church (which seems logical), or something else again, one thing is certain: Such a 'separating' of God's people is definitely on the way.

In early 1995, a New Zealand intercessor was given a powerful vision relating to this. (She believed that it was somehow connected with the effects of 'Toronto'). In this vision, she saw the waters being parted, just as Moses parted the sea. The words that she was given to describe what she was seeing were: "TWO CHURCHES". In other words, what she was witnessing was the dividing of the current church into two totally distinct 'churches' or movements. For a time, while the gap between the two sides was still relatively small, Christians were easily able to jump from side to side. However, as the gap widened, this became more and more difficult, and eventually the only way people could get from one side to the other was to jump into the deep rift itself (the sides of which now looked like huge 'cliffs' of water), to be hauled up by people on the other side.

It is significant to note that right down through church history new moves of God have often brought 'division' and separation amongst God's people. While some Christians have chosen to go with God's true move, others have taken the opposite stance. And from the parables that Jesus told, it seems clear that in the last days, this 'separation' will be far more final and complete than it has ever been before. The time has indeed come for judgment to begin "at the house of God".

In saying all that I have said about Toronto, I do not want to give the impression that I am opposed to every kind of 'unusual' spiritual manifestation. God Himself often does unusual things in times of Revival. But there is a certain 'character' about them that stamp them as being from Him. For instance, tremendous conviction (which is very common in true Revivals) will often bring extreme distress over sin (wailing, weeping, etc), 'trembling' with godly fear, people falling face-down before God, etc. At the same time, the awesome presence of God will often cause those who have experienced His cleansing and forgiveness to be filled with indescribable joy and thanksgiving to God. It is my belief that there will even be "dancing in the streets" (just as David danced before the Lord 'with all his might') in the coming Revival. This may sound strange to some, but such holy, pure and exuberant praise is very common in times of real Revival.

However, what I am speaking of here is very different from the kind of bizarre "casting off of restraint" recently seen in many churches. It is possible to have joy and thanksgiving which is both exuberant and demonstrative, while still being holy and pure. This is the kind of praise that will be seen in the coming Revival. Of course, the new ministries (particularly the musicians) will have to be very careful to warn the people about the dangers of 'soulishness' entering in at this time. This is to be a form of worship that "GIVES" to God, rather than constantly expecting touches or blessings 'FROM' Him. True worship "gives out" to God without expecting anything in return – just because He is so worthy. It is an act of pure and holy 'sacrifice' to God. This is a very important principle.

As I have said before, if soulishness, excesses or counterfeits begin to get out of hand in the coming Revival then it will clearly be up to the leaders to bring correction (though if it is only on a relatively small scale, it may be best not to draw attention to it at all). As well as godly sorrow, holy fear and great joy, we can also expect a genuine outpouring of the Holy Spirit to bring all of the 'gifts' of the Spirit into everyday Christian life: healings, miracles, deliverance, word of knowledge, tongues, interpretation, prophecy, etc. It is also probable that there will be people genuinely "falling down under the power of God" (not that we should ever 'seek' such experiences), visions, dreams, angelic visitations, "signs in the heavens" etc. A large number of these things can be easily counterfeited by the devil, so it will be important to have wise and discerning leaders around, who will know how to step in if things begin to get out of hand. The emphasis of this Revival will be on purity, holiness and evangelism, not the seeking-after of 'experiences'. And everything will be centered around Christ. But it is very important that we do not allow the devil's counterfeits to "scare us off" every kind of unusual manifestation, otherwise we could miss out on what God is doing also.

In forming my opinions about 'Toronto', I have not just stood 'afar off', making judgments about this movement from a distance. Rather, I have personally witnessed these manifestations for myself, as well as speaking with many people who have seen and experienced them first-hand also. None of this has changed my mind, which has been made up ever since I first saw this thing a while ago (at which time every ounce of discernment within me cried out that what I was seeing was not of God). I have seen and read much that is 'pro-Toronto', and have yet to be convinced that any of the manifestations associated with this movement are from the Holy Spirit. In fact, as we have seen, history clearly shows that the opposite is the case, and that this movement should be regarded as a demonic counterfeit, very similar to many such counterfeits down through the centuries.

One thing that has greatly disturbed me about the Toronto movement has been the tendency to simply abandon the practice of 'testing' spiritual experiences and new teachings against the Scriptures. The Bible tells us to "test all things", and of course, there is the well-known verse: "All scripture is inspired by God and profitable for teaching, for reproof, FOR CORRECTION, and for training in righteousness" (2 Tim 3:16). But how can the Scriptures be used for 'correction' if we choose to "explain away" the need for Scriptural proof of our experiences and teachings, etc? If we don't use the Scriptures to 'test' things any more, aren't we opening the door to every heresy, false doctrine or demonic experience in existence? (As history clearly demonstrates). This "casting off" of the authority of Scripture, and the general 'casting off of restraint' that lie at the heart of Toronto, I have personally found to be amongst the most alarming aspects of all. As I have intimated before, there is much that has seemed extremely 'Jezebelic' about this entire movement.

THE PROPHETIC MOVEMENT IN CRISIS

All over the world in the past fifteen years or so, God has been speaking to His people about the great shaking, "change" and Revival that lie ahead. In the USA in particular, this has resulted in the formation of what is loosely referred to as the American 'prophetic' movement, which in many ways, has done an excellent job of informing Christians about the coming great Revival. However, as stated earlier in this book, there have been a number of aspects of this movement which I have to say have disturbed and disappointed me. One of these aspects is the rather mild, 'toned-down' version of the coming "shaking" and judgment that seems to have been preached by a number of these prophetic ministries. To my mind, this has left the people full of expectations of a spectacular 'harvest', but almost completely unprepared for the massive shaking and Reformation of the church which are to precede it.

It surely has to be significant that many who had imbibed the American 'prophetic' message were amongst the first to fall for the Toronto deception (many of them believing that it was somehow 'preparation' for the great Revival to come). Some preparation!

Many Christians may blame the local pastors or church leaders for the spread of this deception. And certainly, God will hold each of them accountable as shepherds of His flock. However, to me, much of the blame for the massive spread of this "Laodicean" deception surely has to be laid squarely at the feet of the prophetic movement. For every prophet is, to a very large degree, appointed by God to be a "watchman on the walls" – to discern and then to loudly warn of any enemy advance. Not only did the current prophetic movement utterly fail to do this, but they actually gave the strong impression that they basically condoned and supported this new movement! Any warnings that they did give were so mild and vague that they had almost no impact whatsoever. Tell me, prophets, is this what God raised you up to do? To go with the popular "Laodicean" flow? I tell you now, the consequences of your compromise at this critical hour may well haunt you for years to come.

Sadly, it is my belief that much of the American prophetic movement is dreadfully under-prepared for the coming upheaval. In fact, it is my belief that very little that it has built will survive the massive shaking that lies ahead. No movement will be immune from the 'sifting' and judgment that I believe God has already begun to visit upon His church. And the prophets themselves, of course, will be no exception.

Tragically, it seems that a large number of today's prophets have found themselves in the position of 'Jonathans' in the current scenario. In other words, they have become caught between their 'reputation' and position in the present order of things, and their desire to be part of the coming 'reign of David'. They have a foot in both camps and they are largely 'acceptable' to both. This is a very precarious (and potentially deadly) position to be in. For as we have seen, because 'Saul' is currently in power, it is far easier to stick with him, than with the outcast Davids. Remember, in the Biblical analogy that we discussed earlier, JONATHAN STUCK WITH SAUL TOO LONG, and ended up falling under the SAME JUDGEMENT THAT CAME UPON SAUL. Even though today's Jonathans have certainly been 'friends of the new move of God', it has clearly been far easier for them to stick with Saul than to risk everything and throw in their lot with the 'Davids'. Such 'Jonathans' are surely now in deadly danger.

It is my belief that it will become more and more impossible to steer a "middle course" between what is of Saul and what is of David today. God will bring about a complete 'separation', a total dividing between these two camps, so that all that is of Saul can fall under the sword of His judgment, and all that is of David can go on to "possess the land" in His name.

Right from the beginning of this book, I have stated my belief that the Laodicean church will have no part in the coming move of God, but rather that a "remnant" coming out from Laodicea will enter into true Revival and harvest. We have already seen how the 'last days' parables of Jesus, and all of Reformation and Revival history, line up with this view. As I have said, I believe that this sifting and separation have already begun. God has begun to 'test' and divide His church. And this shaking is now about to grow much stronger, I believe.

Some time ago, God gave me an analogy from the story of the children of Israel, regarding the "violent faith" that is necessary to truly 'take the promised land'. He showed me that the twelve spies who went in to 'spy out' the promised land were really just like prophets, who have been shown in the spirit what the Revival of tomorrow will be like – a land "flowing with milk and honey". However, in the end result, ONLY TWO of these spies (or prophets) – Joshua and Caleb – had the 'violent faith' necessary to "take the kingdom by force". The other ten spies, even though they had been shown what was to come, simply did not possess the spiritual 'violence' essential to taking what God had promised. Even though they were definitely true prophets (in the sense that they had truly "spied out the land"), they preached an insipid, compromising word, and all who trusted in them perished in the wilderness. Joshua and Caleb, the 'violent' prophets (and their families) were the only ones from that entire generation, who made it through into the promised land. The rest all fell at the final hurdle – the last great 'test'. Their prophets had let both them, and God, down very badly.

What this analogy illustrates is something that is vitally important for all of us to understand also. Primarily, it is that THE KINGDOM MUST BE TAKEN BY FORCE. Mild, insipid, "reasonable" men can never lead the people of God into true Revival. What God really needs is violent, uncompromising "warriors" to lead His people into war – into taking possession of the land 'by force'. Genuine Revivals have always been the most violent, the most controversial, the most revolutionary spiritual events of their day (and this applies even more to the 'time of the end').

What God has shown me very clearly (and this applies to all ministries who hope to have a part in the coming great move of God) is that: It is not "who prophesies wins"; it is not even necessarily "who prays wins"; but rather, it is "WHO DARES WINS". This is the secret to becoming part of the new move of God. For God must have bold, 'daring' warriors to lead His people into the coming great war. "WHO DARES WINS" applies to every would-be Revival ministry. It is simply only those who "dare" who will make it. And it will only be when the new "warrior apostles" arise that this true Revival will begin.

It is my belief that God's original purpose was for the prophetic movement to prepare the way and to welcome in the 'apostolic' move (which will be the move that brings in true Revival). However, things have changed markedly for the worse in the last few years. Ever since the disaster at Kansas in 1991, I believe that the prophetic movement has essentially made little further progress at all towards Revival (in fact, probably none). And any Spirit-inspired movement which loses its momentum in this way soon becomes easy prey for the devil's deception. For the prophetic movement, losing their major prophet/leader Bob Jones was clearly far more than a tragedy – it was an absolute disaster that has had serious repercussions right around the world (but particularly in America).

I have serious doubts that this movement can ever recover from the disasters of the last several years. In fact, historically speaking, movements that get themselves into such a position can be greatly used of the devil to block or hinder what God desires to do next. There is an old saying: "The previous move persecutes the new move of God." And in the current scenario, we would have to say that THE PROPHETIC MOVEMENT MUST SURELY NOW BE REGARDED AS THE "PREVIOUS" MOVE. But is it really possible that elements of the prophetic movement might oppose or persecute the very 'new move' that they themselves have prophesied? Yes, it is possible (it has happened before). The major factor, if such opposition does arise from some existing prophets, will probably be what I call "older brother syndrome" (i.e., envy or jealousy). This has been the hidden motive for much opposition to Revivals in the past, and this time will be no different.

Sadly, it has often been found doubly true of Revivals that "the good becomes the enemy of the best". However, it is my prayer that many existing prophets will see this danger before it is too late, and will avoid this historic pitfall, if it is at all possible to do so.

THE "TIME OF THE END"

I wish to make it abundantly clear at this point that I am not one of those who believe that the triumphant Church will 'conquer' the earth and then deliver it as a kind of gift-wrapped "present" to Jesus when He returns. I do believe that the 'Elijah' ministries will first come and "restore all things" before Jesus returns, as He Himself stated (Mt 17:11. See also Acts 3:21). The Scriptures clearly state that these Elijahs of God will "turn the heart of the fathers to the children, and the hearts of the children to the fathers", before the coming of the great and dreadful day of the Lord (Mal 4:5-6).

I do believe also that, as the Scriptures declare, Jesus really CANNOT return until His enemies are already "made His footstool" or placed 'under His feet' (Heb 10:12-13. See also Acts 2:33-36). However, though I do believe in this period of victory and "restoration of all things" by God's servants, I do not believe that this will be the end of what is to occur in the last days. In fact, I believe that all this will occur immediately prior to what the Bible terms the "Great Tribulation".

Here, briefly, is my own understanding of the sequence of end-time events: Clearly, the first 'theatre' of God's judgment is to be the church. The Scriptures are clear that a time of great "shaking" and testing, of great deception, apostasy and 'sifting' are to come upon the end-times church. It is my belief that it will only be a "remnant" from out of this Laodicean church, led by the 'Elijah' ministries, who will bring in the last great 'ingathering' of souls. This will be the time of the "restoration of all things" (including Israel) that is spoken of in the Bible. Despite this on-going 'harvest' and victory over God's enemies, this will also be a time of increasing conflict, persecution and natural disasters in the earth. However, eventually this 'Elijah'-led move will be utterly victorious. "And they overcame him {the devil} by the blood of the Lamb, and by the word of their testimony; AND THEY LOVED NOT THEIR LIVES UNTO THE DEATH" (Rev 12:11).

Meanwhile, a corresponding war will be fought by God's angels in the heavenlies, against the devil himself and his demons. "And the great dragon was thrown down, that ancient serpent, who is called the Devil and Satan, the deceiver of the whole world – he was thrown down to the earth, and his angels were thrown down with him... the KINGDOM OF OUR GOD and the authority of His Christ have come, for the accuser of our brethren has been thrown down... Rejoice then, O heaven and you that dwell therein! But woe to you, O earth and sea, for the devil has come down to you in great wrath, because he knows that his time is short" (Rev 12:7-12). I believe that this will be the beginning of the "GREAT TRIBULATION" – worse than anything the world has ever seen. It is possible that many of the key 'Elijah'-type ministries, with their main task already accomplished, will be completely taken off the scene at around this time. For, with the devil now expelled from his place in the 'second heaven', and trapped in the earth, the "testing" of the entire Revival movement, and of the hearts of all the inhabitants of the earth will now occur.

What will take place at this time, I believe, will follow exactly the same pattern as the preceding judgment in the church. Great deception will arise, to "deceive if possible the very elect", and all the people of the earth (including those who have been converted during the time of 'harvest') will have to choose between seductive deception and true Christianity. The devil himself will be behind this deception, so it will be very powerful (with 'lying signs and wonders', etc). Only those who "overcome", or 'endure to the end' will be saved. Tremendous persecution will come upon all who refuse to embrace this deception. What dark days these will be! Awful 'tribulation' will be visited upon the earth during this time, because of the devil's great wrath and the judgment of God.

A number of New Zealand prophets have been given dreams and visions of this period. One man was given an incredible vision of the return of Jesus. However, he could also see in his vision that the ground was scarred and blackened, as though some terrible cataclysm had overtaken the earth. My belief is that God will not allow this period to go on for too long, otherwise "no flesh would be saved". I believe that Jesus will return in great glory at this time, with all His angels and all His saints, to finally defeat the devil and his armies at Armageddon, and to cast him into the abyss. "Nevertheless, when the Son of man comes, will He find faith on the earth?" (Lk 18:8). This Scripture gives some idea of how deep and widespread the devil's influence will be at that time. Upon His return, of course, Jesus and His saints will rule over the earth for a thousand years. Glory to God!

What awesome times we are living in! No wonder the Scriptures urge us to remain 'alert', and to be "sober-minded"! It is my belief that clearly one of the major tasks of the new ministries will be to prepare the new converts for the great deception that is to eventually come upon the whole earth. (For these ministries may not be around when it comes). The best way to do this, of course, is to ensure that these converts have an INTIMATE KNOWLEDGE OF GOD, so that they can recognize any counterfeits.

What I have done in the above paragraphs, is seek to give a brief overview of what I believe could well be the sequence of events in these last days. To my knowledge, the above sequence does not do violence to any of the major Scriptural passages on the end-times. Rather, it seems to fit in with them quite well, so far as I am aware. No doubt we will gain further insight into all of these things as time goes by, and as events continue to unfold before our very eyes (as they are already doing now).

IN CONCLUSION

I know that some who have read this book will have found parts of it quite provocative and even shocking in places. However, it was never my intention to 'whip up' controversy, or to offend anyone. What I have attempted to do here is, with as much clarity as possible, faithfully inform and warn all who read this of the great dangers and also the great opportunities of the period that lies directly before us. If I had not spelled out clearly what God has been showing us in New Zealand, then I believe that I would have been seriously remiss in fulfilling the task God has given me.

As I have stated before, it is my belief that we stand today on the verge of the greatest "shaking", the greatest Reformation, the greatest Revival in the history of the church. Truly, for many Christians, this will be the church's 'finest hour'. But it will also be the hour of greatest peril. Only those who "DARE" will win. Many who looked to have the greatest potential will be found to have fallen at the final hurdle, or to have shrunk back from taking their ultimate stand with God. And just because we are not involved with 'Toronto' does not mean that we will automatically enter into the new move of God, either. It is only those who have been truly "revived" themselves who can expect to have a part in the coming great 'harvest'.

I just want to warn the 'non-Toronto' people not to develop a kind of "elitist" mentality, where they assume that just because they have not been deceived this time, they must be one of God's "select few". This kind of foolish pride is just as fatal as any other deception. Only those who are truly humble of heart will have a place in the coming move of God. There is definitely more than one way to miss out!

I would also like to warn the "non-Toronto" people of 'reacting' to this Toronto deception by becoming more and more legalistic, or "anti" every kind of unusual experience. This is exactly what the devil wants (for he loves extremes). I believe that our motto needs to be always, "BALANCE IN ALL THINGS". (Remembering that those who are legalistic seemingly serve a rather 'strict', severe, merciless, 'joyless' God, while those at the "hyper-grace" end of the scale seemingly serve a God who is a kind of 'good-times' merchant, freely accommodating lukewarmness and sin – One whom they need have little 'fear' of at all. Both sides are actually serving a false "God", made in their own image. The truth lies in the BALANCE of both extremes).

The Scripture, "Many that are first will be last, and many that are last will be first", will come into play at every level in this Revival (even amongst the order of NATIONS). The spiritual and cultural 'power centers' of today should not necessarily assume that they will continue to be so. For God is going to use the little and the 'foolish' things of this world to confound and humble the renowned, the powerful and the mighty. There is coming a great tidal-wave of "CHANGE". The old order is about to be overthrown, and the 'new' is to be established by God.

Sadly, in many ways the current situation in the church has reminded me very much of the parable of the 'wise and foolish virgins'. When those who were truly "ready" had entered in, the door was slammed shut, and the 'unprepared' were locked out of the very marriage that they were supposed to be a part of. No wonder there was "wailing and gnashing of teeth"! We are about to see this parable quite literally fulfilled in our day. Tragically, like Esau, it seems clear that many in these days are going to be found to have sold their birthright for a mere "mess of pottage".

As I have already said, the coming days will be truly 'momentous' ones for all Christians. How we respond to the opportunities and the dangers of this time is entirely over to us. I believe that we are about to see a new kind of ministry arise – the 'Elijah apostles', who will rout Jezebel and all her ilk from whatever strongholds they may inhabit, both in the church and in the world, and who will go forth, 'destroying the works of the devil' in Jesus' name, with great daring and resolve. For years Jezebel's influence in the church has been subtle and hidden, but now she has come right out into the open.

It is truly time for God's 'Elijahs' to arise. A great army is about to take the field – hidden and prepared by God for years for this last, dark hour. I believe that the Lord is about to once again be seen as a 'God of war', shaking the nations and scattering His enemies to the dust. We live in the most glorious of days.

I have spoken at length in this book of the 'street-church' that is about to arise, with its anointed repentance preaching, its "new music", and its genuine signs and miracles, etc. I have also spoken of the many 'specialist' ministries that God is about to raise up, who will complement each other with their various giftings, often working in "teams", etc. What a glorious 'Bride' this street-church is to be! No longer will God's people operate from a mindset of expecting the world to 'come to them'. Rather, it will be God's people who will be going out into "all the world". And they will not be making mere 'church-goers' of all nations, but rather true DISCIPLES OF JESUS CHRIST. This will be their heart and their passion. And they will risk everything to accomplish it. These will be a people far more concerned with 'holiness' than with happiness. For them, true happiness will consist of walking in the very center of God's will. Glory to God!

My prayer is that, in some small way, this book will help to warn and prepare all who read it for the awesome days ahead, so that as many as possible might become part of the great thing that God is about to do. His name is about to be glorified in all the earth. And He is inviting many, many of us to be a part of it. Tell me, will you be one who heeds His call?

VISIT OUR WEBSITE-

www.revivalschool.com

HIGHLY RECOMMENDED (ESSENTIAL!) READING:

"Why Revival Tarries" by Leonard Ravenhill.
"Azusa Street" or "Another Wave of Revival" by Frank Bartleman.
"The Autobiography of Charles G. Finney".
"The General Next to God" by Richard Collier.
"Revival" by Winkie Pratney.
"In the Day of Thy Power" by Arthur Wallis.

PLEASE NOTE: There is a much more detailed Bibliography of references and quotation sources at the end of this book.

Appendix

THE END-TIMES VISION OF TOMMY HICKS

by Tommy Hicks

The following is a stunning vision given to American preacher Tommy Hicks (who was a central figure in the powerful 1954 Argentina Revival).

VISION OF THE BODY OF CHRIST AND THE END-TIME MINISTRIES

My message begins July 25, about 2:30 in the morning at Winnipeg, Canada. I had hardly fallen asleep when the vision and the revelation that God gave me came before me. The vision came three times, exactly in detail, the morning of July 25, 1961. I was so stirred and so moved by the revelation that this has changed my complete outlook upon the body of Christ, and upon the end-time ministries.

The greatest thing that the church of Jesus Christ has ever been given lies straight ahead. It is so hard to help men and women to realize and understand the thing that God is trying to give his people in the end times.

I received a letter several weeks ago from one of our native evangelists down in Africa, down in Nairobi. This man and his wife were on their way to Tanganyika. They could neither read nor could they write, but we had been supporting them for over two years. As they entered into the territory of Tanganyika, they came across a small village. The entire village was evacuating because of a plague that had hit the village. He came across natives that were weeping, and he asked them what was wrong.

They told him of their mother and father who had suddenly died, and they had been dead for three days. They had to leave. They were afraid to go in; they were leaving them in the cottage. He turned and asked them where they were. They pointed to the hut and he asked them to go with him, but they refused. They were afraid to go.

The native and his wife went to this little cottage and entered in where the man and woman had been dead for three days. He simply stretched forth his hand in the name of the Lord Jesus Christ, and spoke the man's name and the woman's name and said, "In the name of the Lord Jesus Christ, I command life to come back to your bodies." Instantaneously these two heathen people who had never known Jesus Christ as their Savior sat up and immediately began to praise God. The spirit and the power of God came into the life of those people.

To us that may seem strange and a phenomenon, but that is the beginning of these end-time ministries. God is going to take the do-nothings, the nobodies, the unheard-of, the no-accounts. He is going to take every man and every woman and he is going to give to them this outpouring of the Spirit of God.

In the book of Acts we read that "In the last days," God said, "I will pour out my Spirit upon all flesh." I wonder if we realized what He meant when God said, "I will pour out my Spirit upon all flesh." I do not think I fully realized nor could I understand the fullness of it, and then I read from the book of Joel: "Be glad then, ye children of Zion, and rejoice in the Lord your God: for He hath given you the former rain moderately, and he will cause to come down for you the rain, the former rain, and the latter rain" (Joel 2:23). It is not only going to be the rain, the former rain and the latter rain, but he is going to give to his people in these last days a double portion of the power of God!

As the vision appeared to me after I was asleep, I suddenly found myself in a great high distance. Where I was, I do not know. But I was looking down upon the earth. Suddenly the whole earth came into my view. Every nation, every kindred, every tongue came before my sight from the east and the west, the north and the south. I recognized every country and many cities that I had been in, and I was almost in fear and trembling as I beheld the great sight before me: and at that moment when the world came into view, it began to lightning and thunder.

As the lightning flashed over the face of the earth, my eyes went downward and I was facing the north. Suddenly I beheld what looked like a great giant, and as I stared and looked at it, I was almost bewildered by the sight. It was so gigantic and so great. His feet seemed to reach to the North Pole and his head to the south. Its arms were stretched from sea to sea. I could not even begin to understand whether this be a mountain or this be a giant, but as I watched, I suddenly beheld a great giant. I could see his head was struggling for life. He wanted to live, but his body was covered with debris from head to foot, and at times this great giant would move his body and act as though it would even raise up at times. And when it did, thousands of little creatures seemed to run away. Hideous creatures would run away from this giant, and when he would become calm, they would come back.

All of a sudden this great giant lifted his hand towards heaven, and then it lifted its other hand, and when it did these creatures by the thousands seemed to flee away from this giant and go into the darkness of the night.

Slowly this great giant began to rise and as he did, his head and hands went into the clouds. As he rose to his feet he seemed to have cleansed himself from the debris and filth that was upon him, and he began to raise his hands into the heavens as though praising the Lord, and as he raised his hands, they went even unto the clouds.

Suddenly, every cloud became silver, the most beautiful silver I have ever known. As I watched this phenomenon it was so great I could not even begin to understand what it all meant. I was so stirred as I watched it, and I cried unto the Lord and I said, "Oh

- 149 -

Lord, what is the meaning of this?" and I felt as if I was actually in the Spirit and I could feel the presence of the Lord even as I was asleep.

And from those clouds suddenly there came great drops of liquid light raining down upon this mighty giant, and slowly, slowly, this giant began to melt, began to sink itself in the very earth itself, and as he melted, his whole form seemed to have melted upon the face of the earth, and this great rain began to come down. Liquid drops of light began to flood the very earth itself and as I watched this giant that seemed to melt, suddenly it became millions of people over the face of the earth. As I beheld the sight before me, people stood up all over the world! They were lifting their hands and they were praising the Lord.

At that very moment there came a great thunder that seemed to roar from the heavens. I turned my eyes toward the heavens and suddenly I saw a figure in white, in glistening white – the most glorious thing that I have ever seen in my entire life. I did not see the face, but somehow I knew it was the Lord Jesus Christ, and He stretched forth His hand, and as He did, He would stretch it forth to one, and to another, and to another. And as He stretched forth his hand upon the nations and the people of the world – men and women – as He pointed toward them, this liquid light seemed to flow from his hands into them, and a mighty anointing of God came upon them, and those people began to go forth in the name of the Lord.

I do not know how long I watched it. It seemed it went into days and weeks and months. And I beheld this Christ as He continued to stretch forth His hand; but there was a tragedy. There were many people as He stretched forth his hand that refused the anointing of God and the call of God. I saw men and women that I knew. People that I felt would certainly receive the call of God. But as He stretched forth His hand toward this one and toward that one, they simply bowed their head and began to back away. And each of those that seemed to bow down and back away, seemed to go into darkness. Blackness seemed to swallow them everywhere.

I was bewildered as I watched it, but these people that He had anointed, hundreds of thousands of people all over the world, in Africa, England, Russia, China, America, all over the world, the anointing of God was upon these people as they went forward in the name of the Lord. I saw these men and women as they went forth. They were ditch diggers, they were washerwomen, they were rich men, they were poor men. I saw people who were bound with paralysis and sickness and blindness and deafness. As the Lord stretched forth to give them this anointing, they became well, they became healed, and they went forth!

And this is the miracle of it – this is the glorious miracle of it – those people would stretch forth their hands exactly as the Lord did, and it seemed as if there was this same liquid fire in their hands. As they stretched forth their hands they said, "According to my word, be thou made whole."

As these people continued in this mighty end-time ministry, I did not fully realize what it was, and I looked to the Lord and said, "What is the meaning of this?" And he said, "This is that which I will do in the last days. I will restore all that the cankerworm, the palmerworm, the caterpiller – I will restore all that they have destroyed. This, my people, in the end times will go forth. As a mighty army shall they sweep over the face of the earth."

As I was at this great height, I could behold the whole world. I watched these people as they were going to and fro over the face of the earth. Suddenly there was a man in Africa and in a moment he was transported by the Spirit of God, and perhaps he was in Russia, or China or America or some other place, and vice versa. All over the world these people went, and they came through fire, and through pestilence, and through famine. Neither fire nor persecution, nothing seemed to stop them.

Angry mobs came to them with swords and with guns. And like Jesus, they passed through the multitudes and they could not find them, but they went forth in the name of the Lord, and everywhere they stretched forth their hands, the sick were healed, the blind

- 151 -

eyes were opened. There was not a long prayer, and after I had reviewed the vision many times in my mind, and I thought about it many times, I realised that I never saw a church, and I never saw or heard a denomination, but these people were going in the name of the Lord of Hosts. Hallelujah!

As they marched forth in everything they did as the ministry of Christ in the end times, these people were ministering to the multitudes over the face of the earth. Tens of thousands, even millions seemed to come to the Lord Jesus Christ as these people stood forth and gave the message of the kingdom, of the coming kingdom, in this last hour. It was so glorious, but it seems as though there were those that rebelled, and they would become angry and they tried to attack those workers that were giving the message.

God is going to give the world a demonstration in this last hour as the world has never known. These men and women are of all walks of life, degrees will mean nothing. I saw these workers as they were going over the face of the earth. When one would stumble and fall, another would come and pick him up. There were no "big I" and "little you," but every mountain was brought low and every valley was exalted, and they seemed to have one thing in common – there was a divine love, a divine love that seemed to flow forth from these people as they worked together, and as they lived together. It was the most glorious sight that I have ever known. Jesus Christ was the theme of their life. They continued and it seemed the days went by as I stood and beheld this sight. I could only cry, and sometimes I laughed. It was so wonderful as these people went throughout the face of the whole earth, bringing forth in this last end time.

As I watched from the very heaven itself, there were times when great deluges of this liquid light seemed to fall upon great congregations, and that congregation would lift up their hands and seemingly praise God for hours and even days as the Spirit of God came upon them. God said, "I will pour my Spirit upon all flesh," and that is exactly this thing. And to every man and every woman that received this power, and the anointing of God, the miracles of God, there was no ending to it.

We have talked about miracles. We have talked about signs and wonders, but I could not help but weep as I read again this morning, at 4 o'clock this morning the letter from our native workers. This is only the evidence of the beginning for one man, a "do-nothing, an unheard-of," who would go and stretch forth his hand and say, "In the name of the Lord Jesus Christ, I command life to flow into your body." I dropped to my knees and began to pray again, and I said, "Lord, I know that this time is coming soon!"

And then again, as these people were going about the face of the earth, a great persecution seemed to come from every angle.

Suddenly there was another great clap of thunder, that seemed to resound around the world, and I heard again the voice, the voice that seemed to speak, "Now this is my people. This is my beloved bride." And when the voice spoke, I looked upon the earth and I could see the lakes and the mountains. The graves were opened and people from all over the world, the saints of all ages, seemed to be rising. And as they rose from the grave, suddenly all these people came from every direction. From the east and the west, from the north and the south, and they seemed to be forming again this gigantic body. As the dead in Christ seemed to be rising first, I could hardly comprehend it. It was so marvelous. It was so far beyond anything I could ever dream or think of.

But as this body suddenly began to form, and take shape again, it took shape again in the form of this mighty giant, but this time it was different. It was arrayed in the most beautiful gorgeous white. Its garments were without spot or wrinkle as its body began to form, and the people of all ages seemed to be gathered into this body, and slowly, slowly, as it began to form up into the very heavens, suddenly from the heavens above, the Lord Jesus came, and became the head, and I heard another clap of thunder that said, "This is my beloved bride for whom I have waited. She will come

- 153 -

forth even tried by fire. This is she that I have loved from the beginning of time."

As I watched, my eyes suddenly turned to the far north, and I saw seemingly destruction: men and women in anguish and crying out, and buildings in destruction. Then I heard again, the fourth voice that said, "Now is My wrath being poured out upon the face of the earth." From the ends of the whole world, the wrath of God seemed to be poured out and it seemed that there were great vials of God's wrath being poured out upon the face of the earth. I can remember it as though it happened a moment ago. I shook and trembled as I beheld the awful sight of seeing the cities, and whole nations going down into destruction.

I could hear the weeping and wailing. I could hear people crying. They seemed to cry as they went into caves, but the caves in the mountains opened up.

They leaped into water, but the water would not drown them. There was nothing that could destroy them. They were wanting to take their lives, but they could not. Then again I turned my eyes to this glorious sight, this body arrayed in beautiful white, shining garments. Slowly, slowly, it began to lift from the earth, and as it did, I awoke. What a sight I had beheld! I had seen the end-time ministries – the last hour. Again on July 27, at 2:30 in the morning, the same revelation, the same vision came again exactly as it did before.

My life has been changed as I realised that we are living in that end time, for all over the world God is anointing men and women with this ministry. It will not be doctrine. It will not be a churchianity. It is going to be Jesus Christ. They will give forth the word of the Lord, and are going to say, "I heard it so many times in the vision and according to my word it shall be done."

Bibliography

REFERENCES AND QUOTATIONS

CHAPTER ONE.

1. Source: J.C. Waite, "Dear Mr Booth", pg 19.
2. C.G. Finney. Source: Leonard Ravenhill, "Why Revival Tarries", page 150
3. Source: R. Collier, "The General Next to God", pg 60.
4. Bramwell Booth. Source: Ibid. pg 59.
5. Ref: James Ryle, "The Sons of Thunder" dreams/visions (tape set).
6. F. Bartleman, "Azusa Street", pg 19.
7. "The Autobiography of Charles G. Finney", pg 24-25.

CHAPTER TWO.

1. A.G. Gardiner. Source: A. Wallis, "In the Day of Thy Power", pg 81.
2. F. Bartleman, "Azusa Street", pg 27.

CHAPTER THREE.

1. Rowland Hill. Source: Leonard Ravenhill, "Why Revival Tarries", page 59.
2. John Wesley. Source: R. Collier, "The General Next to God", page 33.
3. "The Autobiography of Charles G. Finney", pg 79.
4. F. Bartleman, "Azusa Street", pg 153-154.
5. John Bunyan. Source: Ibid. pg 171.
6. John Wesley. Source: Ibid. pg 45.
7. F. Bartleman, "Azusa Street", pg 89.

8. Samuel Chadwick. Source: L. Ravenhill, "Why Revival Tarries", pg 26.
9. Source: J. Swaggart, "The Pentecostal Way", in 'The Evangelist', Dec '86, pg 6.

CHAPTER FOUR.

1. F. Bartleman, "Azusa Street", pg 19.
2. Source: Eifion Evans, "When He is Come", pg 55.
3. Source: F. Bartleman, "Azusa Street", pg 34-35.
4. "The Autobiography of Charles G. Finney", pg 82.
5. F. Bartleman, "Azusa Street", pg 69-70.
6. Evan Roberts. Source: David Matthews, "I Saw the Welsh Revival", pg 81.
7. John Wesley. Source: F. Bartleman, "Azusa Street", pg 45.
8. Adam Clarke. Source: Ibid. pg 45.
9. Ibid. pg 152.
10. John Wesley. Source: Ibid. pg 45.
11. A.W. Tozer. Introduction, L. Ravenhill, "Why Revival Tarries", pg 11-12. Copyright (c) 1959. Published by Bethany House. Used by permission.
12. D'Aubigne, "History of the Reformation". Source: F. Bartleman, "Azusa Street", pg 101-102.
13. Source: F. Bartleman, "Azusa Street", pg 46.
14. Humphrey Jones. Source: Eifion Evans, "When He is Come", pg 49.
15. Martin Luther. Source: L. Ravenhill, "Revival - God's Way", pg 15.
16. "The Autobiography of Charles G. Finney", pg 57.
17. Jonathan Edwards. Source: W. Pratney, "Revival", pg 117.
18. Source: Fischer, "Reviving Revivals", pg 84-86.
19. "The Autobiography of Charles G. Finney", pg 105.
20. George Whitefield. Source: L. Ravenhill, "Why Revival Tarries", pg 22.
21. F. Bartleman, "Azusa Street", pg 33.
22. D.M. McIntyre. Source: L. Ravenhill, "Why Revival Tarries", pg 16.

23. Matthew Henry. Source: Ibid. pg 26.
24. L. Ravenhill, "Why Revival Tarries", pg 42. Copyright (c) 1959. Published by Bethany House. Used by permission.
25. A.T Pierson. Source: Ibid. pg 156.
26. John Wesley. Source: Ibid. pg 16.
27. C.G. Finney. Source: Ibid. pg 150.
28. Jonathan Edwards. Source: Fischer, "Reviving Revivals", p. 158
29. R.M. McCheyne. Source: L. Ravenhill, "Why Revival Tarries", pg 33.
30. F. Bartleman, "Azusa Street", pg 81.
31. Ibid. pg 43.
32. A. Booth-Clibborn. Source: Ibid. pg 55.

CHAPTER SIX.

1. John Wesley. Source: G. Strachan, "Revival - It's Blessings and Battles", pg 44.
2. "The Journal of John Wesley", May 23, 1740.
3. C.G. Finney, "Reflections on Revival", pg 66.
4. "Jonathan Edwards on Revival", pg 153-154.
5. F. Bartleman, "Azusa Street", pg 86.
6. Ref: Derek Prince, Personal Update #76, 1995. (Tape).
7. Ref (New Age): C. and S. Grof, "The Stormy Search for the Self". (See also, Christian "SCP Newsletter" volume 19:2, pg 14).
8. Ref: T. Bambridge, "Hypnotism Investigated", pg 93.
9. J. Penn-Lewis, "War on the Saints", pg 150-151.
10. J. Penn-Lewis, "War on the Saints", pg 148.

APPENDIX.

1. Tommy Hicks, End-Times Vision. Source: C. and F. Hunter, "To Heal the Sick", pg 8-16. Used by permission.

Lightning Source UK Ltd.
Milton Keynes UK
UKOW050623070412

190312UK00001B/100/P